RAISE YOUR
INNOVATION
IQ

RAISE YOUR INNOVATION

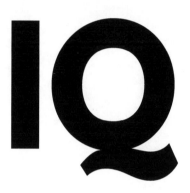

21 WAYS TO THINK DIFFERENTLY
DURING TIMES OF CHANGE

LEENA PATEL

SANDBOX PRESS
LAS VEGAS, NEVADA

Sandbox Press

Sandbox Press books may be purchased in bulk for
educational, business, or sales promotional use. For
information, please e-mail the Special Markets Co-ordinator
at sales@thesandboxpress.com

Library of Congress Control Number: 2019910700
ISBN: 978-1-7332685-1-6
ISBN: 978-1-7332685-0-9 (digital)

PRAISE FOR RAISE YOUR INNOVATION IQ

"Leena Patel has skill, knowledge, flair, and heart."
— Celine Dion

"You have to be willing to do today, what others won't do, in order to have tomorrow what others won't have. Leena Patel is the type of presenter and innovation expert that is doing what others won't do. Her research, knowledge and passion to serve her audiences is second to none. *Raise Your Innovation IQ* moves you to unlock your creative power and then hands you the action steps to future-proof your career or business. If you want to make a powerful imprint in the world – get this book!"
— Les Brown, World's #1 Motivational Speaker, author of *Laws of Success*

"Disruption is happening across the globe and no industry seems immune to it. The question is: What are you going to do about it that will help you thrive and win? I turned to Leena Patel with that question because I believed she could help to fast-track my company's learning and implementation curve. Her strategies are practical, specific, measurable, and actionable. Leena's insights have opened my top leaders' eyes to overlooked areas that are ripe for implementation, after guiding us through just three game-changing strategies. They are here in this book - alongside eighteen others- so that you too can raise your innovation IQ, differentiate yourself in the marketplace, and serve more people."
— Nicholas Bertram, President, GIANT Food Stores

"This is a delightful little book – a fast read, sprinkled with actionable insights and nuggets of wisdom. Don't just read it; share it with your community of doers, innovators and change agents."
— Navin Kunde, Department Manager, Open Innovation, The Clorox Company

"Creative thinking and innovation are the cornerstones of success in today's fast changing business landscape. The strategies outlined in this book are GOLD. You owe it to yourself to pick up a copy and learn the secrets that have helped turn the tide for some of the world's biggest companies."

— Duncan Wardle, founder, iD8 & innov8

"In *Raising Your Innovation IQ*, Leena Patel takes the urgent business of innovation and laces it with serious research and doable actions in a voice that's funny, conversational, and confessional. A game-changer and a treat."

— Jan Sugar, CEO, Sugar Ink

"Leena Patel is my go-to innovation strategist and the world's best kept secret. She has the ability to help you generate ideas and execute on them in a stand out way. In Raise Your Innovation IQ, Leena Patel reveals her secrets to breaking new ground, differentiating yourself from your peers and competitors, and guiding a trend instead of following it...all in an easy-to-read, playful style that makes every lesson stick. Her content, charisma, and humor just jump off the page."

— John Leslie Brown, author of The HARVARD Effect

"Innovation is the most important capability a business can have today. This book will help leaders identify the key competencies and obstacles they face on the path to innovation. Companies that cannot adopt this new line of thinking are destined to become extinct."

— Romy Newman, President & co-founder, Fairygodboss

"The strategies in the book Raise Your Innovation IQ will empower you to lead with skill and heart. I highly recommend reading this book if you want to grow your business with consciousness, while growing your influence and impact."

— Vijay Mehta, Chair of Uniting for Peace and Founding Trustee of Fortune Forum

TABLE OF CONTENTS

FOREWORD

INTRODUCTION

SECTION I: IDEATION

SECTION II: TAKING ACTION

ENDNOTES

FOREWORD

The future of work is unpredictable. Jobs five years down the road don't exist yet. Jobs that exist now may cease to be relevant as technology evolves at a pace we've never seen.

How to stay relevant?

Leena Patel has answers.

Many of today's tools give us the ability to see trend lines, optimize productivity, create cost efficiencies and so on. While tools themselves cannot produce innovation, creativity, and vibrant interactions, our minds do. A great tool, when married with insight and inspiration, can help you build, lead, and innovate.

Raise Your Innovation IQ is a tool that belongs in your rucksack. Clear, concise strategies that will help you to think differently during times of change. Worth keeping handy, along with a pencil and pad as ideas flow from the thought starters and quotes from great innovators.

Leena has a unique perspective borne from an extraordinary life. Many of us have experienced the benefits of her wisdom, grace, and positivity. I've had the pleasure of observing her in her "natural habitat" – in her role as a key part of the most successful production in Las Vegas history – *"A New Day..."* the epic collaboration between Celine Dion and the creator of "O", the inimitable Franco Dragone.

Chaos is ever present in the creation and production of any great spectacle. Enter Leena. Her work preparing Celine for her grueling schedule, ongoing group training with members of the executive management team, and the forty-eight artistes in the show helped each individual achieve consistent high performance. With Leena, we could anticipate a rainbow at the end of any creative thunderstorm. She has literally blown my mind over the two decades that I have known her with the level of skill, thought, and discernment she brings to the table.

In Las Vegas, 21 is a winning number. Let Leena's 21 strategies build your stack!

Randall Jay Irwin
Founder, Departure Creative

"The world as we have created it is a process of our thinking. It cannot be changed without changing our thinking."

— ALBERT EINSTEIN

INTRODUCTION

The number one priority for boards in 2019 is to strategize for challenges beyond the horizon while continuing to drive current business. Ernst & Young believe this duality is "key to surviving and thriving in this period of seismic disruption."[1] Creativity and innovation skills are going to be more critical than ever in business, because nurturing these skills enables companies to stand out in an overcrowded marketplace.

Unfortunately, for the majority, this is no easy task. Our ability to think differently has slowly diminished over the years,. We are certainly adept at driving current business if it requires us leaning on our past experience, however, strategizing for challenges beyond the horizon is another ballgame altogether.

Why is this, and what we can do to change it?

To answer this, let's take a step back and look at a trap that many businesses are falling into: the tendency to overemphasize the role technology plays in their growth potential. While technology is here to stay, what is often overlooked is that *we humans are the ones that have created and steered the technological revolution.* In solving one problem, we have created another. What is most needed *now* is what is severely lacking: the need to bring the human back into technology-driven work environments.

The world doesn't need human beings being doing the work that robots can do. There is enough evidence to demonstrate the psychological damage this has caused. What the world needs now are better problem-solvers, people who bring their whole selves to the table and leverage this strategic advantage to do meaningful work and come up with world-changing solutions. This requires bringing an almost child-like innocence and open mind to our problem solving so that we can see things in ways we have previously never done before.

True story...I was at dinner some months ago with friends, when their six-year-old tugged at my arm while we were eating dessert.
"Aunty Leena...do you have chocolate skin because you eat a lot of chocolate ice cream?"

I was momentarily stunned at his question, and even more so when he pointed to my husband sitting across the table from me, and innocently asked: "Is Uncle

Biren's skin darker than yours because he eats more chocolate ice cream than you?"

I had to resist the urge to quip: "Actually, it's because I like cappuccinos and he prefers espressos", while his father patiently explained to him how people from different ethnicities come from different parts of the world and, over time, their skin responds to the sun differently.

Both mum and dad then turned to us and said, "Thank god you both are like family. That could so easily have been taken the wrong way by anyone else."

How many times has a proud parent relayed to you a story of something clever, or brilliant, or way out of left field, that their child has just said? What has been your typical response? You laugh and admire them for their innocence, right?

"*Kids!*" we exclaim.

We scratch our heads and at the same time marvel at their ability to see the world differently. And then, we get back to the very serious business of being an adult.

For many of us as children, our creativity, playfulness, ability to stand out and say something clever, or be different, outrageous, or unusual was celebrated (or at least accepted) – but as adults, it is often dampened. What changed for us is that we went through the education system to 'learn' and to absorb new knowledge and new skills, and in the process, somehow our capacity to think for ourselves began to shut down.

We were conditioned to toe the line, to fit in. Standing out, being different was shunned upon and ridiculed. We were taught there is a right answer and a wrong answer. We were rarely encouraged to seek out a different answer. We learned to get the answers right in order to fit into a system which rewards accordingly.

By the time we are adults, that creative streak in us that was celebrated and acknowledged and even honored as a child has been shut down. Our inner critic speaks up and says:

You can't think that!
You can't do that!
That won't work!

At work, we have become conditioned to sitting and listening to colleagues conveying information instead of skilled facilitators that invite us to interact with the material in order the drive the lessons deeper. When you apply this conditioning to your business, you can see how it prevents you from taking risks, challenging the status quo, thus gaining that competitive edge in the marketplace.

Now is the time for organizations to commit to nurturing a culture of innovation in the workplace. Innosight reports that the average life-span of S&P 500 companies in 2026 will be only 14 years, with around half of the index being replaced over the next decade.[2]

Whether that scares you or excites you, this book is for you.

The time is ripe for you to develop what will become your super-power in business — the ability to think differently and rise above the noise. To do this, you'll need to ask bold questions and entertain solutions and responses that challenge the status quo – just like my friend's six-year-old kid did.

Thus, as we begin this journey together, here is my *Chocolate Ice Cream Challenge* for you:

Be more *daring*, more *courageous*, more *curious*, and more *playful*.
Be like a kid in a sandbox.

Your willingness to change the way you think will open up a whole new world of possibilities.

As of the writing of this book...and according to Fast Company, here are the World's Top Ten Most Innovative Companies in 2019[2]:

1. **Meituan Dianping**...*for pioneering transactional super apps*
2. **Grab**...*for leveraging transportation to create a super app for SouthEast Asia*
3. **NBA**...*using streaming that has democratized the sport*
4. **The Walt Disney Company**...*for delivering their own streaming service*
5. **Stitchfix**...*for reinventing retail*
6. **Sweetgreen**...*for emphasizing its roots*
7. *Aspeel Sciences*...*for keeping food fresh longer*
8. *Square*...*for making online payments less painful*
9. *Oatly*...*for commercializing a milk alternative*
10. *Twitch*...*for making live streaming mainstream*

Now, look at who topped the list in 2018[3]:
Apple, Netflix, Square, Tencent, Amazon, Patagonia, CVS Health, The Washington Post, Spotify, and the NBA.

Did you notice that only two of the companies maintained their place in the top ten? While this list is not the *only* list that recognizes innovation, it gives a glimpse of how challenging it is for companies today to maintain their edge. Big companies need all the nimbleness of a start-up in order to maintain their marketshare. And with the right positioning, young startups can quickly transform their respective industries and take the big guns out of the game.

Whether you are part of a big business or a young startup, my question for you is ***how are you going to raise your innovation IQ so that you keep adding value to the marketplace in new and exciting ways?***

Specifically:
1. *When* will your company be on this list?
2. *How* are you going to improve your positioning over the long haul?
3. *What* will you stand for at the height of your success?

You're Better At This Than You Think

Think back to the lunches or dinners you've had over the past week.

Do you recall at any point thinking *I'm going to eat X... actually, no...I'll have Y instead?* Maybe you started off thinking you'd have pasta, and instead, decided to order the chicken with a side salad.

If you experienced this...congratulations! **You CHANGED YOUR MIND!**

We are often deeply resistant to change because we like the comfortable and familiar – even though we encounter new information and new experiences all the time.

If you're wondering how to overcome this resistance and be more responsive during times of change, here's a tip...

Make Thinking Differently Your Expertise

In this fast changing world, you need to balance having expertise (which brings with it a level of predictability) with the ability to think differently (which brings it with fear, chaos, and uncertainty).

To get better at thinking differently you need to improve how you think. To improve how you think, you need to be conscious of your instinctive patterns and when (and how) to switch to a new one when needed. You need to empty your mind of the old so that it has room for the new.

A subtle distinction: Make thinking differently your expertise, not thinking differently so that you can increase your current expertise. Once you are armed with strategies on how to think differently, you will go on to apply them to *any* situation.

When you embrace this shift, you will become a better problem solver, and when you become a better problem solver you add more value to the world. It won't be limited to the confines of your expertise, which means you'll be able to connect the dots in ways others haven't been able to. You'll be able to innovate faster.

HOW TO READ THIS BOOK

This book is designed to raise your consciousness, give you a nudge in areas you may be holding yourself back, as well as teach you strategies on how to free your thinking so that you can raise your innovation IQ.

While the journey is an exhilarating one, it can also be overwhelming. With that in mind, while I recommend you start at Chapter One, you do *not* have to read the rest of this book in sequential order. While later chapters reference terms in earlier chapters, you'll catch on to the terminology pretty quickly. Fear not! Start off with what resonates or draws you in. Dive in where you feel inspired. The beauty of a book in this format is that you *can* zig-zag.

As you read, you'll notice that ideas will intersect. This is intentional. I am training you to get better at seeing the bigger picture and connecting the dots between innovation 'niches'. While I wanted to put links in places where I cross-reference to make it easier for you navigate your way around, not every format allows for this. Maybe innovations in publishing will make this easier for authors in the coming years. Until then, you'll benefit from going back and re-reading previous chapters as you go through the book so that you can absorb the lessons more deeply and explore the intersections for yourself.

Then, apply them to your own business challenge to create your own super innovation roadmap.

While new ideas are sparking away in your brain, know that you are honing a skill that will enable you to play an integral part of your company's drive to envision and execute on ideas that will change how we experience and interact with the world. It's an exciting journey for the willing and daring, and I'm honored you are taking me with you on yours.

One final note: This book is an amalgamation of ideas drawn from a variety of industries as well as past experiences that I have had. I hope that by allowing me to indulge a bit and start off by sharing some background, you too will see how your life story is every bit relevant to the role you are in today and that your diverse experiences are integral to your ability to think differently than everyone else.

You can do this.
Now is your time.
See you in the sandbox,

Leena Patel

P.S. Every strategy in this book ends with an action step that is designed to get you immediate results. If you do the work, you'll reap the rewards.

Now, let's get to ~~work~~ play...

SECTION I:

IDEATION

"...many things have a plurality of parts and are not merely a complete aggregate but instead some kind of a whole beyond its parts..."

— ARISTOTLE

#1

POLISH YOUR INNER POLYMATH

Polymath :

a person of wide-ranging knowledge or learning.

Imagine breaking bread with Aristotle, Leonardo da Vinci, Pythagoras, Michelangelo, and Alexandra Graham Bell. These people have been celebrated for having expertise and deep interest in a wide range of topics from art and science to literature and politics. The conversation could go in so many different directions as their insights and experiences from an array of fields would intermingle, collide, fuse, and, I'm sure, spark new ideas and theories.

While today, we have access to more information than at any point in history, some might argue we are also in an era of widespread ignorance. Most of us are simply too busy to spend hours learning how to paint and speak another language, while pondering unified field theory, string theory, general relativity, the latest developments in climate change, and the balance between the conflicting creative energies Apollonian and Dionysian that Nietzsche espoused in *The Birth of Tragedy*.

But *what if* we made the time? What if by doing so you would perceive the world we live in more accurately than everybody else? Would this give you a competitive advantage in business?

Without a doubt.

Most people learn one discipline like management or software or accounting or computer science, but the innovators are the ones that integrate multiple disciplines and make connections between unrelated fields. That's where the quantum leaps happen.

Elon Musk has tied together physics, programming, design, engineering, technology, and manufacturing in his quest to bring electric cars to the masses and commercialize space flight. His ability to make connections between different fields gives him an extreme edge. Today, every major car maker in the industry – Mercedes, Porsche, Audi, Ferrari, and others are following his lead and getting their plants ready to produce electric cars.

Steve Jobs combined innovation with design, technology, marketing, hardware and software and it enabled him to think light years ahead of the competition. His study of calligraphy, the influence of Buddhist philosophy, and his passion for music are all well documented, and it's not a leap to see how this as translated into beautiful craftsmanship, the simplicity and clean design of the Mac, and the launch of iTunes.

And, if you don't mind, I'll take a moment here to share my journey here too...it's relevant, I promise.

The Unfolding

As a young child, I was greatly influenced by my grandfather — a lifelong mentor to me. He was a direct disciple of Gandhi. Grandfather met Gandhi at the age of sixteen when he came to deliver a talk at grandfather's school. From that moment on he knew his life's purpose and dedicated himself to supporting Gandhi's vision of bringing independence to India through non-violent means. Grandfather stayed with Gandhi in his home. He went to his prayer meetings. He read books that Gandhi advised him to read. As a result, our family grew up being immersed in Gandhi's philosophy.

I was introduced to various scriptures from an early age, including Gandhi's discourses on *The Bhagavad Gita*, the ideas of Thoreau, and the practices of yoga and meditation. As a teenager, I learned about social activism, servant leadership, and how to influence and lead change. I studied and practiced Buddhism for twelve years and was appointed Young Womens' Leader of a lay Buddhist organization at the age of sixteen, supporting over one hundred other young women in their professional and personal growth.

I memorized the stories my grandfather would tell me of Gandhi's struggles in South Africa and India, the leadership of Winston Churchill in Britain and the rivalry between him and Gandhi. These are all experiences that have stayed with me. They have, without a doubt, shaped who I am and how I lead others today.

In college, I studied Cognitive and Quantitative Psychology and had it not been for my love of the arts, I might have ended up having a private practice somewhere. Instead, after a fateful evening seeing

London Contemporary Dance Theater perform at Sadler's Wells Theater in London, I chose to pursue a career in dance. I was a soloist in a pop-rock band named Joi in the nineties and one of my memorable career highlights was opening for Annie Lennox and Dave Stewart for their European Peace Tour. All in all, ballet and modern dance for me was a powerful vehicle that taught me how to communicate without having to use my voice. Ironic, given that today I speak and train others to speak up and use their voices to influence others.

After I retired, I entered the world of coaching and began training athletes and entertainers. I worked with artistes like Jaime King, training her to do her own stunts in the movie *Bulletproof Monk*. I worked with Celine Dion to get her physically and mentally ready for *A New Day*.... I coached the gymnasts, trapeze artists, clowns, and synchronized swimmers at Cirque du Soleil. I worked with filmmakers and actors. I worked with leaders in creative and non-creative sectors alike. I taught them how to use their body and voice to communicate to audiences with power and authority. I taught them the Russian Ratchett – a system for driving elite performance that Olympic athletes used to win championships – and applied the concept to product innovation to help teams generate fresh ideas. I integrated the yoga and mindfulness practices I had learned from my grandfather and my study of Buddhist philosophy into my repertoire to help leaders cultivate deep presence when the stakes were high.

One concept I learned in my college psychology class resonated with me the moment I heard it: **gestalt**. Translated it means:

The whole is greater than the sum of its parts.

During this time, *gestalt* was a guiding principle for me. I somehow felt that the dots were connecting in a bigger and more meaningful way than I could imagine for myself at the time. I just had to trust the process.

Creating a Latticework of Mental Models

Consulting and training world-class athletes and performers in entertainment, sports and media gave me a new set of distinctions around creativity, elite performance and business growth that I went on to apply when I opened up my consulting practice to other sectors.

The diverse combination of skills I had accumulated allowed me to excel in a role that demanded mastery in a multitude of arenas: executive coaching, stage performance, sports, entertainment, design, storytelling, innovation, psychology, and more. I had created a latticework of over a dozen mental models, with more still to come.

During this time I was exposed to the business of innovation in sectors ranging from healthcare and media to technology and retail. I learned how to translate creative ideas into a tangible ROI. I learned how data, marketing, design, personal branding, leadership storytelling, and the nurturing of an inclusive workplace culture were all integral to the growth and success of a company. I learned how to see the big picture, the gestalt, as well as the micro-level details that went into nurturing an organization that is world-class, innovative, leading-edge, ground-breaking, and financially lucrative.

The Birth of Gamulation: Connecting the Dots Between Games, Game Mechanics, and Simulations

My next breakthrough came when I started exploring the intersection between the fun, play, and competitive component inherent in sports, games and game mechanics (goals, progress, status, and rewards) with the world of simulations in order to accelerate the learning and development rate of employees and enable them to become more strategic and profitable.

Games + Simulations led to the creation of *Gamulation*: an innovation in instructional design that particularly appeals to the new generation of leaders that enjoy interactive, immersive learning experiences. The methodology enables the learning of core business skills in a way that engages the senses and appeals to our love of fun and adventure. By looking at how people learn, engage with, and process new data, and combining this with the changing needs of the marketplace I inadvertently stumbled upon what has become our secret weapon and the one thing that differentiates us from all the noise in the innovation space.

This innovation took my firm, Global Impact Systems, to a new level of impact and revenue within a year. I developed and ran 45+ gamulations both to USA audiences and internationally – which generated a ton of new data – which, in turn, spurred further innovations. On one occasion, for instance, we collaborated with a Womens' Business Resource Group to deliver a gamulation that would help them understand the value of team communication and inclusion. The women, between them, generated two hundred and fifty new ideas that the company could implement right away. Three of those ideas were quick wins that could be built out and implemented within the same financial year that led to a forty percent increase in the company's bottom line.

This led to the realization that large organizations don't always have an integrated innovation strategy in place, meaning the company's growth plans and innovation initiatives are separate from, for instance, the company's diversity and inclusion strategy. So we've been penetrating this space and helping leaders in some of the world's biggest companies leverage their underrepresented talent to drive further innovations.

In recent years, I have been fortunate to have been commissioned to design and deliver customized experiences for clients that teach teams lessons in Product and Process Innovation, Sales and Marketing, Strategic Thinking, International Negotiations and Diplomacy, Presentation Skills, Climate Change and Sustainability, Communication and Conflict Resolution, Team Building, and much more. And because of my background in arts and entertainment and my love of music and design, every learning experience pushes the envelope in terms of creativity. I look to surprise and delight people. I want to evoke an emotional response. When people are emotionally invested, they'll be more engaged, which means they'll remember the lesson after the event, and will be more driven to take action.

All this to emphasize:

Your life story is every bit relevant to the role you are in today, and your diverse experiences are integral to your ability to think differently than everyone else. Embrace them wholeheartedly.

"The future," as Ernest Boyer, United States Commissioner of Education anticipated decades ago, "belongs to the integrators."

Forget Being A Specialist

The biggest mistake I see people make is that they get stuck in one worldview or theory. They perceive the world through a singular lens.

They become analysts, or researchers or digital marketing experts – and they shut off the parts of their story and background and experiences that are key to the blossoming of bold new ideas. They make sense of the world by making sense of the "part". They don't take time to see the "whole".

For some, it is as if their job description tells them to do X and so they have cast aside every other mental model they have ever come across that doesn't doesn't align with X in order to fit in. Many of these people are acting on autopilot. They know – but they have forgotten that they know. They need reminding. Others have not made these connections for themselves – or have never thought about making these connections. They don't know – and they don't know that they don't know. It is as if they are asleep. These folks can be woken up. They can be taught and they can be trained. Once they connect the dots and risk taking new action as a result...watch out world!

Success is seeing the gestalt. It's about seeing the ins and outs of dozens of different world views and skillsets – and then seeing where they intersect in order to create new theories, paradigms, models, inventions, and breakthroughs. It's about creating a latticework of different mental models and connecting the dots between them all.

ACTION STEP

Look Outside Your Industry

Are you facing a challenge that you can't seem to solve using your old methods? You may have become so specialized in your thinking and approach that it has stifled your creative problem solving ability. Look to outside experts from other industries to give you some fresh input and insights.

"Study the science of art. Study the art of science. Develop your senses — especially learn how to see. Realize that everything connects to everything else."

— *Leonardo Da Vinci*

Take On Three New Subjects

Take the Polymath Challenge: Make it your mission to learn the ins and outs of three new subjects over the next three years. Michael Simmons defines a modern polymath as 'Someone who becomes competent in at least three diverse domains and integrates them into a top 1-percent skill set'.[4] You don't have to invest ten thousand hours into mastering the subject, but don't be a dabbler either. Your goal is to develop a level of knowledge in each so that you can hold your ground in an in-depth conversation with a subject matter expert.

Connect The Dots

Did you play an instrument when you were in school? Love tinkering with apps? Enjoy video gaming? Did you have a previous side hustle as a disk jockey? Have a passion for the environment? Here are some of my expert skills, deep passions, interests, and life experiences - expressed as a crossword puzzle.

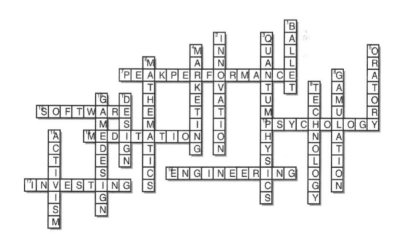

Let it spur you to think about the intersection of the various dots in *your* life. What ideas have you exposed yourself to in one place that you could apply to your current situation?

Create Your Own "Theory Of Everything"

Physicists have attempted to create a "theory of everything" so that they could better understand the world and why things occur the way they do.

Attempt to create your own "theory of everything" by tying your various areas of expertise and interests all together and exploring their interconnections. The best business leaders in the world create their own worldview and constantly reinvent themselves because of the new information they are processing, filtering, and integrating so they can stand out in a crowded marketplace.

Is there a connection you can make that no-one else has spotted? Is there a breakthrough idea in you that could create a brand new field or industry where there is little to no competition?

Don't Think You've Got It In You? **Think again.**

When I work with organizations to help their people brainstorm and problem solve, again and again, the teams are amazed at the literally hundreds of ideas that they are able to generate between them in the space of a few days. Then comes the work of filtering these ideas and integrating them into business operations and the marketplace in a standout way.

I've witnessed it so many times now, I can say with a high degree of certainty – this ability to polish your inner polymath exists in you. In fact, if you've ever been accused of having too many interests, you may already be on the path to being one without realizing it.

Trust that this ability, while not common, is not impossible to develop either.

For many of you, it is lying dormant and needs the right soil and fertilizer to bring it out: The soil is the company you work for and the culture they create. You provide the water and the sunlight by cultivating the discipline to follow through on building the diverse set of skills using the techniques, ideas, and guidelines I have outlined in this book. The fertilizer is surrounding yourself with the right advisors and mentors to help you channel these ideas into a high-value skillset.

"There is a vitality, a life force, a quickening that is translated through you into action, and there is only one of you in all time, this expression is unique, and if you block it, it will never exist through any other medium and it will be lost...It is your business to keep it yours clearly and directly, to keep the channel open."

– Martha Graham

Need some inspiration?

Expand your circle of people you spend time with to include people that come from different backgrounds, that think differently to you, and that won't automatically reaffirm everything you already believe. Have lunch with a different person every day and take the time to learn what makes them tick. Allow them to intellectually challenge you. Tear down walls by being genuinely curious.

The future belongs to the polymaths. Putting a plan in place to learn more about new subjects and bringing your past experiences to your current role will give you a huge competitive advantage. While none of us can predict with absolute certainty what the future holds, during times of change we can, should, and must prepare for it by making an investment in polishing our inner polymath and connecting the dots in our life in a way that no-one else can.

"The real key is to live in an environment where the mind feels free to choose the right thing instead of being compelled by habit and inertia to choose the wrong thing."

– DEEPAK CHOPRA

#2

UN-HABIT YOURSELF

The first step in changing how you think is becoming aware of what your default is. Each of us have, over the years, developed a framework for how we diagnose problems, and our gift and our downfall is this: it tends to be built around our expertise, acquired knowledge, accumulated experiences, and innate way of looking at the world. This in turn translates as an addiction to a singular viewpoint – or what I call *category preferences*.

The Story of Bacterium

One of the most well-known examples that demonstrates this occurred in the healthcare industry when a group of bacteriologists discovered a bacterium that they thought caused stomach ulcers. Gastroenterologists, however, resisted the finding for a decade. Since *their* worldview up until that point was that bacteria could not survive in the gut, they had no previous history of studying them. Because of this limitation, they had developed category preferences.

In fact, the bacteriologists had to get creative in their branding so that their radical discovery could gain acceptance from other doctors who did not feel comfortable publicly admitting their mistake. When the bacteriologists coined it 'a new class of disease', it finally gained acceptance from other doctors.

My Experience

We surround ourselves with people who think like us because different thinking threatens our identity. My own experience has confirmed this for me. When I first got introduced to Kolbe profiling and took the Kolbe Index assessment, I discovered I am what is called a *Quick Start Initiator*.

The assessment results affirmed for me the following:

You are uniquely able to take on future-orientated challenges. You lead the way to visionary possibilities and create what others said couldn't be done. You'll say "yes" before you even know the end of the question – then turn it into a productive adventure.

While I already knew I was a natural innovator, it didn't dawn on me that my strength also had its own shadow. I had a tendency to hire team members who were just like me, that thrived on coming up with never-done-before ideas. But – like me – they often didn't have great follow through and were not always skilled in helping me take great ideas to completion.

Without this awareness, when I came across someone who took their time to think things through, who didn't catch on to visionary ideas quickly, but instead needed spreadsheets and flow charts and Venn diagrams in order to make sense of things, I would struggle to connect with them. Now my response to such a person tends to be *"A-ha!' I am totally nabbing that person. They've got a skill I lack."*

I've discovered that these types of thinkers can be organizational mavericks who challenge me to take a fresh approach to projects. By embracing their category preferences instead of being attached to mine, they're going to play an integral part in taking our company vision (or a client's vision that we have supported them in developing) to seamless completion. This is how I have strategically built out my trusted team who support our company growth and every consulting project we undertake.

Change is happening so fast around us today, that how and what you were taught to think carry their own limitations and liabilities. Flexing your awareness muscle to un-habit yourself takes conscious practice. It requires you to be mindful of *how* you are thinking or doing *while* you are thinking or doing. It requires you to witness yourself and your thoughts, preferences, judgments, beliefs, actions, and reactions so that you can decide for yourself if they serve you. If they don't, you now have the ability to choose new frameworks and ideas that do.

ACTION STEP

Become more aware of your category preferences and develop **_category consciousness_** by putting yourself into situations that expose the singular elements of your thinking. This will enable you to grow multiple perspectives.

Engaging in role-play can be helpful, and often enlightening. So can walking a mile in another person's shoes. Try shadowing team members for a day and living a different response. Get comfortable with dissonance, welcome contrary opinion, realize where your preferences and biases lie and how they are limiting your professional performance in the workplace. See what comes up that shakes your worldview and regard it as an invitation to thinking differently.

Ask yourself the following questions:

- *How do I view situation X?*
- *How do I arrive at conclusions?*
- *What about my background, education, experiences, or upbringing is influencing how I arrive at this conclusion in this moment?*

- *How does my methodology differ from the way others arrive at their conclusions?*
- *Which lens am I looking at this problem from?*
- *What happens if I change the lens?*
- *Is my way the only way?*
- *Am I absolutely sure that X is true?*

Use these questions to heighten your consciousness around your preferences over and over until the internal questioning becomes a new habit. This new habit will gift you with the experience of a new kind of freedom. You will no longer be the same person, confined to your old ideas about who you think you are, what you are capable of, and what you can – or cannot – do. You will be better equipped to address category conflicts when they arise, and you will be on the rich and rewarding journey of un-habiting yourself.

"If you don't jump on the new, you don't survive."

— SATYA NADELLA

#3

PREPARE TO PIVOT

Pivot :

a sudden shift in strategy that can turn a mediocre idea into a billion-dollar company.

A pivot occurs when a company makes a sudden strategy shift after recognizing that a product is failing to meet the needs of its intended market. A pivot can take place because customers needs have changed, or because of external changes such as new technology or a changing economic climate. Whatever the shift, if you look closely enough, being prepared to pivot will enable you to tap into new opportunities during times of change.

The Listerine Story

From Surgical Antiseptic to Mouthwash

For decades after Listerine first entered the market in 1879, it was a jack-of-all-trades product; the surgical antiseptic that could be used to scrub floors, clean feet, and treat medical conditions such as gonorrhea.

That changed in the 1920's – an era that saw the birth of companies targeting consumers' desires and fears in advertising to influence buyers and drive purchasing decisions.

...Boosts Your Popularity and Lands You A Husband!

Tapping into women's anxiety that they would never get married, Listerine mouthwash made the shift to portraying bad breath as an embarrassing medical condition that urgently required treatment. The pivot boosted sales and grew brand loyalty with zingers such as: 'Halitosis makes you unpopular'[5] and bold claims such as it being a superior product that would prevent bad breath 'four times better than any tooth paste.'

Ads advised consumers *Every night...before every date, make it a habit to use Listerine.* How could anyone not?

The Post Story

Before The Great Depression, Post was the consumer cereal brand of choice. Launched in 1897, the cereal dominated the breakfast-eating world until the 1930s. Then hard times set in, and Post – believing that they dominated the market – cut back on advertising spend, braced themselves for a slow economy, and hunkered back to weather the storm.

Little did they know a hungry tiger was lurking in the shadows...

While Post retreated, their competitor – a small, relatively unknown organization called the Kellogg Company – made a quick pivot: they began doubling their ad spend[6] with merry slogans like 'Snap! Crackle! Pop!' At a time when the country was at an emotional low, Americans gravitated towards the cheery messaging and sales began to grow.

Kellogg also sent a clear message that they were invested in people. They became one of the first companies to display their cereals' recipes and nutritional info on their packaging — so consumers knew exactly what they were eating.

Loyalty for Post declined and Kellogg's became the go-to cereal company of choice.

Whatever you do, don't ignore the signs

Kodak at one time was the market leader in photography and film, and was positioned to be the pioneer of the future. They created the digital camera technology yet misunderstood the ways that consumers wanted to interact with their photos. They were soon wiped out by competitors who innovated on their pioneering products and filled the niche that Kodak created, yet failed to capitalize on.

In many respects, ignoring the signs of what was happening in the marketplace is what lead to the downfall of Kodak. As leaders, it is vital to pay attention to the signs and not just get comfortable doing what you have always done when your marketplace you are operating in has changed.

Many businesses today are operating like Kodak, not realizing the grave cost of not rolling with the times, and not taking the time to understand the changing needs of their customers.

Zig When Everyone Else Zags

Innovation is about zigging instead of zagging.

It is about making a bold move to say *YES* to a change in direction while your competitors are doing what they have always done.

It is about being on the alert for the next big opportunity. It is about obsessing about your customers and their needs, likes, desires, habits, and more.

It is about redefining their current experience and, indeed, giving them what they want before they even know they want it.

Did you know that both Facebook and Youtube started out intending to be dating sites?

That Groupon began as a fundraising platform before it entered the local coupon business?

That in the early days, PayPal started as a way to send money between mobile phones, Palm Pilots, and pagers?

That Nintendo was a manufacturer of playing cards for the Japanese market?

These companies were prepared to pivot so that they could take advantage of bigger and better opportunities. Lots of companies find themselves in a situation in which their current business is not, or is no longer, hitting the mark. Yet many respond with inertia. **Change happens. When it hits, be prepared to reassess and quickly switch gears.**

ACTION STEP

Prepare to pivot in times of fast growth and rapid change – or when your business is not getting the growth, or is falling short of the targets you have set.

Here are four ideas on how:

1. **Pivot to Focusing On ONE Feature.** Is there a feature of your product or service that you can put the spotlight on and make a core element of your messaging? Increase your impact by figuring out a way to really make this feature stand out.

2. **Pivot to A New Target Demographic.** Could college students be an untapped, lucrative path? Or professional women? What about millennials who love to travel?

3. **Pivot Your Business Model.** Instead of direct to customer, have you explored working with a distributor or a value-added-reseller? Does moving from retail storefront to e-commerce make sense? What about the subscription model? the membership model? the free-to-premium app model?

4.   **Pivot to Embrace New Technology.** Can you digitize your operations or processes? Automate your inventory? Self-optimize production? Is acquiring a young, fast-growing tech company a viable strategy?

Now is the time to evaluate opportunities and solutions in order to improve your capabilities and capture greater market share. Don't wait for a crisis to hit before you take action

...and if a threat is looming, **act fast.**

How will you choose to

pivot

during times of change?

"Learn the rules like a pro, so you can break them like an artist."

— PABLO PICASSO

#4

BREAK THE RULES

There is not *a single industry that has not experienced disruption in some shape or form...*

Think physical stores disrupted by e-commerce.
Public libraries disrupted by Wikipedia.
Newspapers disrupted by online blogging.

Instead of email, we text.
Instead of picking up the phone, we update our Facebook status.

We file taxes online, rather than hire accountants.
We have access to online legal forms which reduce our need for basic legal advice.
We can apply for a mortgage via an automated lending process...without ever talking to a loan officer.

No longer is pitching to a venture capitalist firm or a group of investors the only option. Today, we can fund a start-up with crowdfunding.

And it's not just industries. Countries too.

Data localization policies in Brazil, Russia, China, the European Union, India, Indonesia, Korea, Nigeria, and Vietnam and other countries are disrupting US firms that rely on international trading for the survival of their business.
India is experiencing the growth that Japan once had.
China is fast becoming the powerhouse that America has been.

And the list goes on.

At its extreme, disruptive change has given birth to new business models, overhauled operations, and generated innovative products that have changed our lives. It has toppled tycoons and corporations. And it has made multi-millionaires of founders of start ups that have their eyes and ears open for the next big thing – and are nimble enough to act on it.

These shifts are not happening overnight; rather, they are gradually creeping up on us.

If change is moderate, urgency becomes less apparent

If you got into a hot tub and the temperature changed from 63°F to 93°F in the span of half a minute, you would notice the difference. In fact, you would probably feel the extreme change in heat by the time it was 80°F – if not before. However, if the temperature change was gradual, you would be less likely to notice it. In fact, the temperature might creep up and up, and you might be comfortable staying there until it reached 93°F – simply because *you didn't realize you were over-heating*. This is because we have a heightened sensitivity to shocking change.

If change is moderate, urgency becomes less apparent. Before we know it — we're fried.

The lesson is...

Be on the lookout for the rulebreakers that are instigating the smallest shifts as well as those that are massively disrupting your industry. Those shifts could be through the release of a new product or a response to a change in legislation, or simply pivoting to embrace a new feature, business model, technology, demographic, or business model.

Rules that inhibit new thinking

As we talked about in Un-habit Yourself, we are oftentimes constrained by our own experiences and expertise. However, it isn't just our own thinking that gets in our way. The corporate environment also has its own set of established rules by which we operate.

We're too big.

We're too small.

We can't do that.

That won't work.

We don't have the resources.

I'm not senior enough.

We've already tried and failed.

I'm not allowed to do that.

We're just starting out.

We're too far along.

Who am I to make a decision like that?

That's the way we've always done it here!

Do any of these sound familiar?

Duncan's Story

When Duncan Wardle was the head of Innovation and Creativity at Disney, his team was asked to develop a game-changer idea for Walt Disney World. To address the challenge, the team listed all the rules of going to Disney World:

- A guest has to book a hotel room.
- A guest must buy an entrance ticket.
- A guest must stand in line to enjoy the rides.
- A guest meets the characters.
- A guest buys food.

They picked one rule to break – "Guests have to stand in line" – and then brainstormed a list of rule-breaking questions.

- What if there were no lines at the resort hotel?
- What if there were no turnstiles at the theme park entrance?
- What if guests never had to wait in line to get on a ride, or meet their favorite character, or pay for dinner?

Breaking the 'have to stand in line' rule led to the creation of the MagicBand.

The MagicBand wristband acts a room key, entrance pass, credit card, and a databank of all the ride reservations guests have made in advance – including giving FastPass+ access to all the experiences. It completely eliminated the need for visitors to stand in long lines.

By breaking just one rule they had previously lived by, Wardle's team gave Walt Disney World visitors a better experience which translated into increased spend at the park. The innovation also enabled Disney to collect data that they can use to improve the guest experience in real time as well as enhancing the development of future offerings.

Here's the deal:

At any given time you are either breaking the rules, following someone else's rules, or you are completely out of touch with what the rules are.

The first gets the largest rewards.
The second gets an honorary mention.
The third eventually goes out of business.

Recognize the need to break the rules and commit to ongoing change so that you are not in a tier you don't want to be in. **Even small shifts disrupt markets and disruptors know that rules are made for the masses.**

ACTION STEP

A Two-Word Hack...

Of course, our limited thinking will surface. We are human after all. To overcome this, having a shortcut up your sleeve helps.

Here are the two magic words to keep top of mind:

What If

The next time you catch yourself playing by the rules, ask yourself:

What if this wasn't true?
What if it was and it didn't matter?
What if I found a way anyway?
What if you could solve X?
What if the rules no longer applied?

What if Steve Jobs did not have a vision of a world where computers governed our lives?
What if Square hadn't extended the benefits of banking?
What if Slack couldn't wrap its head around the idea of making inboxes obsolete?

What if Instagram didn't create a platform which enabled the world to share beautiful photos?

How different would our world be today?

How can you apply *What If* to your situation or challenge?

This is when your trusted strategic advisors and team members can be of great help. **Gather everyone together and brainstorm ideas.**

"The trouble with having an open mind, of course, is that people will insist on coming along and trying to put things in it."

— TERRY PRATCHETT

#5

PRACTICE NON-ATTACHMENT

A friend of mine, Nicholas, is a great fan of Burning Man. When he came back from last year's festival, he giddily explained the impact the event had on him and his friends. One of the things I found most fascinating about his account was how much creativity is generated at this event. The event is a platform for self-expression and freedom from judgment.

There are people that have spent the entire year working on huge art installations – everything from a steel sculpture of a woman, 55-feet-tall and lit by 3,000 LEDs, to a group of enormous rainbow mushrooms made out of corrugated plastic. And at the end of the event, do you know what they do with them?

They burn them.

"They clean up and pack up their things and return the desert to its state of vast emptiness, as if Black Rock City and all it contained had been a mirage."
— Brian Doherty, *This Is Burning Man*

"It's not about the result," Nicholas explained. **"It's about the creative process. It's about falling in love with the *doing*.** We enjoy the fruits of our labor for the time we have to enjoy them. Then we let go."

The practice of burning their art teaches artists non-attachment to the outcome or results of their efforts and is a nod to their spiritual journey of eradicating personal feelings of fear and self-doubt. For my friend, burning his art was a symbol of the death of his suffering.

"What if there was no attachment to a particular outcome?" he asked. "There would be nothing left to fear and so there would be no more suffering."

You might be thinking: "That's crazy talk, Leena! This is serious business. I'll get fired if I don't produce results.

How can I be expected to meet my goals without being attached to the outcome?"

Here's the distinction...

When it comes to innovation, this is about practicing non-attachment in order that you may get out of your own way. This is about letting go of your preconceived notions of *what* can or can't be done, *why* something should or shouldn't be done, and *how* it can or can't be done. It is about letting go of old ideas of right and wrong. It is about releasing all *shoulds, can'ts, won'ts,* and other self-defeating vocabulary – whether spoken out loud, or as a passing mental thought.

While you need to set clear objectives, and attain certain results in order to meet the commitments you have made, your challenge is to empty your mind before you do the work of setting targets, outlining steps, holding yourself accountable to results.

Without an open or empty mind, you might unknowingly be attached to results that don't actually serve you or your company, which means you can easily end up making stupid decisions.

Psychologists call this phenomenon the **sunk-cost bias.**

If you've ever held on to a pair of shoes that make your feet ache or a pair of pants that no longer fit you for no other reason than you paid a lot of money for them, you've experienced the sunk-cost bias.

It's the tendency we have to continue investing time, energy or money we have *already* invested into a losing endeavor – *just because it has already cost us something.*

No-Mind

The Japanese call this state of openness *mushin or no-mind, i.e. A mind that is not fixed or occupied by thought, and thus, open to anything.*

Both followers of Zen and the Dao embrace the concept of *mushin.* They believe this state is achieved when our mind is free from anger, fear, or ego during everyday life. In these moments, we are judgment-free. Practicing *mushin* in the workplace will enable you to get more skilled at thinking differently.

Meditation, mindfulness, Zen, Buddhism, the Dao, A Course In Miracles, and a multitude of other spiritual practices and disciplines have been a core part of my life since I was four. I grew up living and breathing these practices. Hence, the action step for *Practicing Non-Attachment* is a powerful technique that draws from my lifelong immersion into these various disciplines. I've used it myself for decades, have taught it to thousands of others, yet have never shared it publicly before. Until now.

I call it the ***ALTTA Process***.

ACTION STEP

THE ALTTA Process

To utilize this process effectively, it is helpful to put yourself into a state of openness and be in a quiet environment where you can really listen. I prefer to be sitting down during this process because it helps me feel more grounded, but once you master it, it can be done anywhere and anytime you need some perspective.

You are about to embark on an inner dialogue with your higher self and seek silent counsel from the universal wisdom available to you in the deepest recesses of your own consciousness. Kinda like a single wave tapping into the power of the ocean, a cloud merging into the expansiveness of the sky, a teeny tiny single cell tapping into the other one hundred billion cells that comprise your brain.

The ALTTA Process comprises of five steps and the word *ALTTA* is an acronym.

Ask

Listen

Trust

Thank

Act

Let's break these five steps down...

Step 1 – Ask

Ask for guidance on anything you want clarity on. If you think your category preferences or your internal stories are getting in your way and your monkey-mind is getting dizzy with analysis, ask the universe or a higher power to lead the way.

Mentally ask for guidance or for clarity:

Should I follow plan X or Y?

What is the best approach with X?

If you don't know what to ask, ask: *'What would you have me know now?'*

Once you've asked the question, be still and...

Step 2 – Listen

Listen for the answer. Really listen. This means putting aside all preconceptions, judgments, beliefs, desires, wants, and limited ideas of what is and is not possible. Suspend your own conclusions and ask your bigger, infinite mind for a perspective greater than your own. Then, be open to what answers emerge.

At this stage, you are gathering insights from more than your five senses and going beyond your own best, most logical, reasoning in order to tap into the deepest and highest part of you. You may receive an answer in the form of a word, a feeling, an impulse, an expression, or an idea. Get out of thinking mind and listen to your feeling body. Pay close attention to how you feel while you're feeling it.

Don't decide what you should be feeling in advance. Decide in advance not to decide, and instead, simply listen. You don't need to strain to listen. Relax. Be patient. Be still. It will come. This takes practice in the beginning because your mind will want to pipe up with your preferences which may not truly serve you.

Once something lights up, it will feel like an aha, a eureka moment, an intuitive knowing. Resist the urge to react. Don't do anything except...

Step 3 – Trust

Trust that the insight or idea or answer that lights up for you is exactly the right answer for you. Don't second-guess yourself. Don't argue with the answer. Don't analyze it – at least not right now. Allocate a separate time for that if you need it afterwards. Acknowledge that your knowledge has its limitations and you don't know everything there is to know.

Get out of your own way by trusting the revelation. It may not make sense to you. Your conscious mind might want to kick and scream and wrestle with the guidance. Whatever you do, don't ignore your higher self.

Imagine a wave relaxing into itself, being a part of the natural ebb and flow of the tide...without you having to do anything. Be like a wave.

This is the time to trust that the universe is conspiring in your favor.

Step 4 – Thank

When you feel a sense of peace and have put your trust in the insight, mentally say *Thank You.*

This puts you in an immediate state of gratitude.

If you are familiar with the Law Of Attraction, you'll know that what you put out into the universe, you receive back in spades. If you express thanks for clarity, you'll get more clarity. It's as if the universe has heard you, has given you this guidance, has given your desire to see things differently a heightened energy, and now, as you give thanks, it showers you with more.

More clarity. More peace. More ease the next time you do this process.

You'll find that all your conscious and unconscious questions around who you are as a leader and creator, how you show up, what action you take, and what you stand for can be answered with this process.

The simple act of thanking and being in a state of gratitude will change the way you look at things forever.

Step 5 – Act

The final step in the ALTTA Process is to take action.

Faithfully follow the instructions. It will likely feel daring, ridiculous, and downright scary. Especially if the stakes are high.

Start with small things until you gain confidence. Over time it will get easier. Promise.

I have coached thousands of people in this process and I have seen it change lives and transform the decisions leaders make in business - especially when things get tumultuous. **Trust the process and take bold action.**

It really will
ALTTA you!

A Word of Warning...

The **ALTTA Process** is simple to learn but takes diligent practice to master. Persevere. Once you "get it", it is like receiving the key to the kingdom. It can be used for *any situation or scenario* where thinking differently is needed.

Did I say 'Act' already?

Let me know how you get on with the process. Send me a tweet @LeenaPatelLive using ***#ALTTAProcess #IIQ*** *and I'm happy to share more insights and dialogue with you about your experience. I'll also share stories about my own sunk-cost bias mishaps that happened when I* ***didn't*** *turn to this process.*

"Either you run the day or the day runs you."

— JIM ROHN

#6

CALENDAR UNSTRUCTURED TIME

William McKnight, President and Chairman of the Board of 3M for thirty-seven years, was a visionary in his perspective on people and innovation. He believed in the motto "Hire good people and leave them alone."

After spending many of its early years struggling financially, 3M launched the 15% Program in 1948[7]. He encouraged employees to set aside 15% of their work time to proactively cultivate and pursue innovative ideas that made them light up. While they still had the responsibility of ensuring their day-to-day responsibilities were executed upon, employees were gifted with paid time and space to think creatively and hatch their own ideas that challenged the status quo. Whether it was developing a more streamlined way to run a process or experimenting with cutting-edge technology, the *15% Culture* – as it became known at 3M – gave employees freedom to exercise their initiative, push boundaries, and solve new problems.

Several innovations have come out of the 15% Culture including Multilayer Optical Film, Cubitron™ Abrasive Grains, Emphaze™ Flash-Free Adhesive, and Post-It® Notes. Today, with well over 100,000 patents filed,[8] it is key to the company's innovation strategy.

The practice caught on...

3M's 15% Culture has inspired big companies like Google and Hewlett-Packard Labs to follow suit. These companies recognize that innovation needs time to develop and when people are busy putting out fires and chasing short-term goals, creativity will be dampened.

When I visited the Google campus in Mountain View, CA for a lunch meeting with one of its VPs, I had an opportunity to witness a bowling alley, meditation pods, dance classes, and the slide employees jump on to take them from one floor to the one below. I immediately felt that play, fun, creativity, and balance of mind and body were integral to the high performance of employees. It was clear that the environment was created in this way because Google's leaders recognize that when people dedicate time to play at work, their right brain is engaged, they are more in flow, and are more likely to innovate. And I could see the pride employees had in working in such an environment.

Calendaring time for unstructured time sends the brain the message that playtime is a vital component of idea generation and fresh inspiration. It gives you permission to be in a state of discovery without purpose or agenda.

"Playtime is a vital component of idea generation and fresh inspiration. It gives you permission to be in a state of discovery without purpose or agenda."

Leave Some Grey Space

Many companies communicate an unspoken rule that play doesn't belong in the workplace. As a result, we feel guilty for allowing grey spaces on our calendar because it conjures up fear that we are neglecting our responsibilities.

"If I see grey space, I MUST fill it with a meeting," one of my C-suite clients, David, told me.

We were in the middle of an Executive Strategy Day with the leadership team. The others had left the room for a quick break so David and I had a few minutes to ourselves.

"David, what's your company's top priority this year?"

We had just spent the entire morning determining what their organization's top priorities were, and were about to outline their game plan for accomplishing them when the others returned. So while I knew the answer, I asked the question intentionally so he would have to respond out loud. Sneaky.

He cocked his head to one side as he mentally recapped the morning, the various ideas that had been thrown up on the whiteboard, and what they had committed to.

"To scale the organization," he responded. "Our plan is to open up in two new regions this year."

"And how will you do that if your schedule is so packed that you don't have time to solve the inevitable problems that will come with growth? How will you have the bandwidth to think strategically about your ventures or to execute? How will you put out the fires that will come up?

You can't do it. Well you can do it because that's what years of experience has given you. Mastery. But you shouldn't be doing it.

As this company scales, your role is going to evolve with it. You'll be hiring new people which means you'll need to train them."

I paused to take a sip of water, while the words slowly sank in. David listened, his hand resting under his jaw. I could see he was still struggling with the idea.

"If you want your leaders to take the reins and competently handle things," I gently explained, "you are going to have to teach them how to address challenges without your constant input.

David nodded, understanding. "That makes a lot of sense."

"You don't need more meetings," I concluded, seeing the others starting to file back in. "You need to reallocate how you spend your time, and you need to calendar in unstructured time."

Leave the grey space

on your calendar.

You're going to appreciate having the available time to sit and focus on strategic growth. You're going to appreciate having the extra time to process all the new data and information coming your way.

Take 30 minutes, or an hour here and there, to train and support team members as needed, but as you ramp things up, you're going to REALLY appreciate having this scheduled time to breathe and just

BE.

Thinking Differently And The Limbic System

Does it surprise you to know that thinking differently is not entirely dependent on your IQ?

Cognitive psychology tells us there is a connection between how we think and our emotional state and it's all taking place at the base of the brain, in the limbic system9. The limbic system is responsible for processing external stimuli, determining the emotional significance of a situation, and controlling our response. It has the power to open up our ability to make new and novel connections as well as shut down access.

When you are under stress, on a time crunch, or feel pressure to create, your ability to form new connections and apply new knowledge is reduced.

Chemicals are released which inhibit the flow of complex thinking. They cause your mind to go blank and to feel stumped, which puts you into flight mode, makes you want to scream *I Don't Want To Think*, and shuts down further playful exploration.

ACTION STEP

Commit to making *thinking differently* a core value. Echo it in your company culture by allocating employees regular unstructured time to explore passions and interests that will not only rejuvenate them, but also has the potential to generate breakthrough ideas and new revenue streams.

While dedicating 15% of your time might not be a luxury your company can afford right now, the principle can still be applied on a smaller scale. As a leader, experiment with your team members calendaring one afternoon a week to pursue something they have discovered through the usual course of work but haven't had the time to follow up on.

Remember: the best ideas can come in a flash, but are most likely to surface when our mind – and calendar – has room to breathe. When you calendar unstructured time, your limbic system is no longer blocking the flow of signals to this region of the brain which means it is supporting you in raising your Innovation IQ.

If your company or team leader doesn't allocate you time, consider making the business case for testing it out over the course of a few months as a pilot project. Ensure you commit to tracking how the time is spent and what new trajectories you take when in this free-flowing state. What gets measured, gets mastered.

Of course, dedicating intervals for unstructured time will only be truly effective if the executive leadership team are willing to champion new ideas that emerge out of it. However, in the right environment and implemented skillfully, it is a great way to unhinge your "inner geek."

...And you never know...**your idea could be the next million-dollar idea the world (your company) is waiting for.**

"Everybody is a genius. But if you judge a fish by its ability to climb a tree it will live its whole life believing it is stupid."

— ALBERT EINSTEIN

#7

GET CREATIVE WITH DATA

Data, used wisely, enables you to gain insights that can help in making strategic decisions. It enables you to see where you are heading, where you have been successful, and what still needs to be done, thus, furthering the goal of improving business performance, productivity, and profits. In today's environment, data and analytics have become central to innovation in product design, marketing, servicing, risk management, and much more.

The danger with data is that it can seduce you into remaining stagnant. When you are getting data that affirms what you are doing is working you may be less likely at this stage to take the risk of saying *Let's switch gears and try something new...*

The Achilles heel of big businesses today is the value placed on engaging in deep analysis before inching forward in a new direction – often a daunting proposition for analytical, data-driven people. For these individuals, the urge to keep collecting data becomes a strategy for avoiding change; paralyzing them and preventing them from breaking new ground.

I recently spoke with a senior global leader at one of the top financial institutions in the world. As we were discussing a new training program for her leadership team that was part of a bigger plan to draw more women into executive leadership within their organization, she said to me:

"We're looking for something new and different. We've experienced the traditional approach that the big firms are offering and we want something that goes beyond this. We also love data. So anything you bring us has to be grounded in data for us to consider it."

This leader wanted an approach that was cutting-edge and unique, and that stood-out from the norm, yet it needed to have gone through enough testing or analysis to make the executive team feel safe enough to take a chance.

So how do we go about achieving this goal of incorporating both creativity and data into our solution?

Answer: We **Get Creative With Data.**

Lean On Personal Insights

Art director, Matt Vescovo, was the creative genius behind one of the comical Sauza Tequila ads. His billboard ad shows a guy opening a fortune cookie after eating a Chinese meal.

The message on the cookie reveals:

> # That wasn't chicken.

And underneath, reads Sauza Tequila's trademark slogan:
"LIFE IS HARSH. Your tequila shouldn't be."

While Vescovo didn't rely on a research report to find out if people would get the joke, he did lean on insights he had personally collected over the course of his life. His practice is to allow his brain to go back and forth between the need for creativity and data. "The right brain comes up with the creative idea and then the left-brain fact checks it,"[10] he says.

The ad was a winner in the US. [And luckily Vescovo's left brain did kick in and his right brain didn't lead him to designing the ad to run in India. Imagine an ad image showing a bowl of half-eaten minced beef curry and the fortune cookie message reading "That wasn't lamb."...]

The Creativity, Data/Risk-Management Conundrum

Not everyone is a data lover and not everyone is a natural creative. I'm not saying you can't have, or develop, the ability to do both. I recognize that much creativity is needed in data analysis, and vice versa – however, one will reign supreme for you over the other. There are arenas of our ability that we will naturally quantify as a level 8, 9, or 10 and arenas that we will score lower.

Think about what happens when you decide to cook a dish you've never made before...

Are you comfortable with experimenting and trying out new recipes without knowing the outcome?

Do you need to read the recipe or follow a video or watch a demonstration before doing anything?

Or are you happy to skim through the list of ingredients, look at the picture, and then begin the process, knowing that you can get help as you go along if you need it.

I used to dislike following recipes of any kind. I felt like it was stifling my creativity. I learned to cook by feel and taste and, early on, developed a level nine knack for figuring out which flavors blend well together without reading a cookbook. A pinch of this and a sprinkling of that...and don't ask me how, it just works.

Then I fell in love with baking bread and making homemade pizza and pasta and desserts. (I'm a glutton for chocolate molten lava cake!)

I quickly discovered that if I put too much yeast in, or omitted the salt, or mixed the dry ingredients with the wet at the wrong time, my culinary goodies would come out looking or tasting weird.

So I trained myself to follow recipes where utmost precision is required. While today, I am more patient and have learned to find joy in a task because it supports my end goal (eating delicious food that is not loaded with preservatives or sugar) I'd probably still only score myself a five at this skill. It's not likely to become my default. If you ever come over for dinner, be prepared for a culinary adventure. However, unless I make homemade bread, pasta, or chocolate molten lava cake, please don't ask me for the recipe afterwards.

We each have instinctive ways of thinking and problem solving that will feel natural to us, yet may be viewed as alien to our colleagues. How you intuitively respond to fact-finding and analysis, or to documenting processes and developing repeatable systems, will give you a clue as to where you sit on the Creativity – Data/ Risk-Management Continuum.

CREATIVITY - DATA/RISK-MANAGEMENT CONTINUUM

In order to look at aligning these different ways of thinking and problem-solving from a creative angle, let's dive deeper into these two instinctive types. I call them:

Intuitive Creative Thinkers
(ICT)

and

Intuitive Data/Risk-Management Thinkers
(IDRT)

The Intuitive Creative Thinker (ICT)

Creative professionals often wear their dislike for data like a badge of honor. It is common for creative teams to see research and data as soul sucking creativity killers...as barriers that stand in the way of their big ideas.

Some of you reading the statement above will consider yourself a natural or intuitive creative and will resonate strongly with it, much like I did many years ago when it came to baking and being forced to follow a recipe. As an ICT, you are the type of thinker who will help your organization or team generate bold ideas that will take them into the future and stop them from become dinosaurs in the industry. Organizations need you!

You are also the kind of person who favors instinct over research. If this is you, know that you still are drawing on data — it's simply more likely to be data you've collected through experiences and observation over the course of your lifetime versus consumer data. Keep in mind that drawing on the latter will help feed your brain with new ideas. Make data your ally. Instead of fighting it, view it as fuel to spark new thinking.

When used correctly, data is not the enemy of Intuitive Creative Thinkers; it is a powerful friend.

The Intuitive Data/Risk-Management Thinker (IDRT)

If you have a love of data and statistics, you are likely a person who:

- prioritizes managing risk over big ideas that haven't been tested and proven
- favors research over instinct
- excels at keeping an organization or team from making costly mistakes
- loves spreadsheets and checklists!

Organizations need you.

Just keep in mind that this strength of yours may, at times, stop you from being open to new ideas and easily embracing a new, different, untested approach.

ACTION STEP

Do THIS if you are an Intuitive Creative Thinker (ICT)

To validate a concept and get buy-in on your idea(s), it will serve you to **create and run through a rigorous internal checklist**.

Ask yourself:
- Do other people agree with this, or is it just me?
- How many times have I seen X come up?
- How many times have others mentioned to me that X is not working for them?

When you start tracking the responses it is going to keep the creative part of your brain from floating off into la-la land and enable you to more quickly get the validation you need to see your ideas come to fruition.

Do THIS if you are an Intuitive Data/ Risk-Management Thinker (IDRT)

If you're an Intuitive Data and Risk-Management Thinker, your goal is to **think differently about *how* you access data**. Keep analysis simple and focused.

You now have permission to sit behind your keyboard and play cultural anthropologist. Tactically dig out valuable details about your audience or market such as trends, topics, brands and publications they follow, words they use to describe themselves, hashtags they use, memes they post, etc. Intentionally start gathering new information that allows you to open your mind to generating new ideas and connecting dots in new ways. Then, allow rapid prototyping and market testing to guide your analysis and decision-making.

For ICTs and IDRTs

Create strategic collaborations
Consciously bring together Intuitive Creative Thinkers (ICTs) and Intuitive Data and Risk-Management Thinkers (IDRTs) into a single team to leverage each other's strengths. You each can become the other's most powerful ally – providing your former nemesis(!) with the very thing that is holding them back.

- **ICTs** – Collaborate with data analysts who are true problem solvers. Before they start tapping into a statistical or computer science algorithm (because that's the way they've always done it) invite them to identify possible causes of model failure. Then use your talent to help them brainstorm solutions.

- **IDRTs** – Collaborate with creative professionals who live inside their imaginations, yet need to gather data to support their ideas and solutions. Listen to their ideas and then use your talent to support in validating – or playing Devil's Advocate – to their suggestions.

Increase awareness of your instinctive competencies and category preferences to help you to recognize why roadblocks come up. Balance your complementary energies and use the power of gestalt thinking to stay aligned with the company vision and overcome conflict as it arises. By asking powerful questions and challenging your current practices, you will make your entire team better, stronger, and more efficient.

Get Personal With Your Team!

To learn more about your team members' instinctive capabilities, reach out for information on two conative assessments we can administer: *Kolbe* and *Think Six*.

"Ninety percent of this game is half mental."

— YOGI BERRA

8

RACK UP SINGLES AND DOUBLES

When Michael Eisner took over Disney, the company was losing money. One of the immediate measures he took was to avoid spending an excessive amount of money by using expensive A-list celebrities. Instead, he focused on coming up with good movie ideas and making them with a low budget. His vision was to find talented actors who had fallen from grace, or television actors (instead of film stars) that would command a lower fee.

Singles and Doubles is a baseball metaphor where singles and doubles are the terms used for getting on first and second base respectively.

In terms of projected revenue, lower budget movies – based on their allocated production and marketing budgets – are more likely to produce Singles or Doubles. Mid-budget films target revenue comparable to Doubles and Triples. And the big budget movies would go after the big money; Home Runs and Grand Slams.

While a Single or Double doesn't excite the crowd the way hitting a home run would, they add up and are often critical to winning a game.

With big-ticket actors out of the equation, Disney movies under Eisner's leadership could generate *Singles or Doubles* revenue levels and still be profitable. They no longer had to do really well to turn any kind of profit –-or in baseball terminology – make Triples, Home Runs, or Grand Slams.

The Singles and Doubles approach played a major role in the turnaround of The Walt Disney Company in the 1980's where a flop on a large scale could have easily ruined them financially. If it resulted in a big hit, it netted a high profit.[11]

Disney opted to hire television actors Ted Danson and Tom Selleck instead of film stars in the American adaptation of *Three Men and a Baby*. The film grossed $167 million in the domestic box office with an $11 million budget[11]. The Singles and Doubles strategy paid off handsomely.

Ultimately, without the pressure of box office success, Disney could take bigger risks and invest in innovative storytelling. The result was that after just four years under Eisner's leadership,

Disney became the #1 studio in the industry, with operating income jumping from $300M when he joined, to $800M.

Today, with increased competition, the pressure to hit a home run for businesses is higher than ever. Disney addressed this by changing strategies and going for the home runs and grand slams by bringing in bigger talent and creating higher-budget films like Dick Tracy, Armageddon, and Pearl Harbor – but they did this only when the company was on more solid financial footing.

Screen Gems' Story

Screen Gems, a mini-major film production and distribution studio, followed this exact strategy and made a killing.

The 2016 production budget of their horror movie *Lights Out* was $4.9M. The box revenue generated was...

Wanna take a guess?

It was **$148,768,835.**[12]

That's a 3036% ROI.

Not too shabby.

Interestingly, former President Barack Obama also leaned on this analogy when speaking at a news conference in the Philippines in 2014:

"You hit singles, you hit doubles; every once in a while we may be able to hit a home run.

But we steadily advance the interests of the American people and our partnership with folks around the world."[13]

In doing so, he was making the point that he preferred the United States deploy every possible economic and institutional lever before resorting to armed force. He knew it would enable him to **avoid errors and make slow, steady, progress.**

There's a time for setting big, hairy, goals and there's a time for micro milestones. Your micro milestones, when strung together, can really add up. However, if you are always going for that home run, your attempts are more likely to become outs. It can be better strategically to go for *Singles and Doubles* and make modest wins most of the time, rather than to hit those home runs *some* of the time.

Unless your company is on solid financial footing and you are comfortable taking those bigger risks, the *Singles and Doubles* approach can be a winning strategy that can keep your revenue growing slowly and steadily. **It may not be sexy. It may not be a media magnet. But it will move you closer to your goal while allowing you to sleep at night.**

ACTION STEP

Map out a strategic plan for the next twelve months to include 1-3 epic wins (outcomes that are bold, daring and visionary), as well as small milestones (wins that take some hustle but are achievable).

Ask yourself:

- What objective(s), if and when achieved, would classify as a *Singles or Doubles* win?
- What objective(s), if and when achieved, would classify as a *Triple* or a *Home Run* for you?
- What is involved in achieving each of them?
- What are the risks and hurdles of each?
- How will you divide your energy for the next quarter? 6 months? 12 months?
- What are the key results that will tell you you are on track to successfully execute this strategy?

"What man dare, I dare:
Approach thou like the rugged Russian bear,
The arm'd rhinoceros, or the Hyrcan tiger,
— Take any shape but that, and my firm nerves
Shall never tremble."

— MACBETH, ACT III, SCENE IV

#9

DARE TO SUCK

Dare :

To have the courage to put forward, as an idea, especially when rebuff or criticism is likely.
To confront or oppose boldly.

The best advice I got from a mentor was to be brave in spite of my self doubt, shame, and anxiety. To rise to a challenge and risk falling flat on my face in the process. And since he had a sense of humor, he condensed the essence of his counsel into three words and put them up in bold capital letters on a flip-chart:

DARE TO SUCK

Little did I know that these three words embedded in my psyche would play a part in changing my business model and how I would connect with my clients and trainees going forward.

It was the first time I was asked to get up and do a skit in front of an audience at an improv night. If you've never been to an improv night, think of *Who's Line Is It Anyway?* Now imagine YOU are in the spotlight with the pressure on to come up with something clever or witty.

Outside, I was STRONG and confident.

Inside....

... this is how I felt.

I nervously walked on to the stage and stood in the spotlight. People did this for fun?

I was given a scenario that I had to respond to about five seconds before my time began.

"You have just received a phone call with some terrible news..." boomed the host over her microphone. "Aaaaand...Go!"

I picked up my imaginary phone...

And then it happened.

Every speaker's worst nightmare. My mind went...

BLANK.

Eeeek....!

I couldn't think of a single word.
I couldn't think of a scenario.
I couldn't think of one single example of bad news.

I stood on stage with a stunned look on my face, my mind searching for words, ideas, a storyline...*anything*. I didn't say a word for close to two whole minutes. The audience's eyes were glued to me. My feet were glued to the floor.

You could have heard a pin drop.

Miss-Quick-Wit-With-A-Come-Back-For-Everything is finally at a loss for words. I felt like a complete idiot as I imagined the audience thinking the worst.

When the timer went off, the audience erupted.
"I was on the edge of my seat," one participant told me afterwards. "Your expression told me it was the worst news ever. I was dying to know what you had been told. The suspense was killing me!"

It turned out she was an event planner. She was so impressed that I could hold people's attention for two minutes without saying a word, that after a brief exchange about my firm and our areas of expertise, she asked me if I was available to speak at an upcoming event.

Being the rookie that I was, I confessed my boo-boo.

"Didn't you just see me *suck* on stage? There is *no way* was I am cut out to be a speaker. Are you *sure* you want to pay me to speak on your stage?"

"It didn't matter. You didn't let it show. We all thought it was intentional. If you can hold the audience's attention *without* speaking, I can't wait to hear what you have to say when you *do* speak."

So I spoke at her event.
And I loved it.
And the business leaders in the audience loved it and got a ton of value from it.
And that's how I fell in love with public speaking.

After that speaking lowlight, I spoke as often as I was invited, and I got better and better. Today, I speak in front of hundreds of people on an almost weekly basis without batting an eyelid. I am on the faculty for a global speaker training company that trains business leaders how to tell their leadership story and get their message out into the world in a more powerful way. And I get invited to speak at conferences around the world and deliver strategic insights and help more people to win at innovating. Speaking to large groups enables me to do that effectively because it leverages my time.

What kept me going back on stage in those early years is knowing that I had already done the one thing that people fear most about public speaking: freezing on stage.

And I had survived. Everything else had to be a piece of cake.

Fast forward to an event I was invited to speak at last year...

I was invited to lead a training for a government organization last year in which I broke up the heavier content-based instruction with a fun, interactive knowledge-based quiz. I gave attendees ten questions and a list of ten answers and they had to match up the correct answer to the question. That means that there were only ten possible answers to each question, and since many of them knew the answers to approximately one third of them and they were in small groups, putting their heads together and taking a guess at the rest would give them pretty good odds that they would raise their score by a couple of points. Or that's what I thought.

Here's what actually happened...

Every single group only matched up the answers they knew – and even after I playfully suggested, "Take a guess with the remaining ones...what d'ya have to lose?!" – *not a single person did.*

They were so afraid to be wrong that they didn't give themselves permission to fail, to even take a guess...and this was during a light-hearted quiz where the results didn't even matter!

That's how afraid we are to be wrong.

The underlying issue here is self doubt...and all self-doubt stems from fear.

We fear we're going to be found out.
"What if I'm not as good as they think I am...?"

We fear being thought of as stupid.
"What if she laughs at me?"

We fear feeling inadequate.
""What if this bring up all my other insecurities and I end up a blubbering mess in front of my colleagues?"

We fear making a mistake.

"What if I get the answer wrong?

Such thoughts can haunt you and prevent you from taking chances, in business, and in life. When you feel all this fear – no matter where it stems from – you also become averse to risk.

If you are not prepared to take risks, make mistakes, feel your fear and take a bold step forward anyway...*you'll never come up with anything original.*

ACTION STEP

What really helps to move the needle when thinking differently is to give yourself permission to make mistakes. Screw-up. Make colossal boo-boos. Get comfortable with being imperfect. Dare to suck. Mistakes are part of the journey towards making a big breakthrough in innovation.

Learning environments that don't support you in 'getting the answer wrong' prevent you from taking risks and challenging the status quo, – the very qualities needed to gain a competitive edge in the marketplace.

Ask yourself:
What is the best case and worst case outcome that could come out of this?

If you're okay with the worst, then there is nothing stopping you. And if you're not, put some strategies in place to mitigate the risk.

Great leaders realize that sometimes they're going to be right and sometimes they're going to be wrong – and they're okay with that. Great leaders make the best decision they can in the moment and course-correct when they make a mistake. And great leaders learn the lesson so any mistake made is not repeated. While change is never easy, adhering to the *Dare To Suck* principle can lead to a fresh perspective, a new outlook, and a renewed connection to ourselves and to life. Daring to suck requires a mindset shift.

What would you do if you knew every screw up you made would take you one step closer to where you need to get to?

Would you be braver?
Would you dare greatly?
Could you nod your head in acknowledgement of your shame and do it anyway?

The Bottom Line... Don't let fear of making mistakes paralyze you from taking action. Give yourself, and others, permission to fail. You never know...just like it did for me, your (perceived) epic failure might be the very thing that leads to your next biggest breakthrough.

P.S. In researching and writing this book, I have since learned that Theatre of Ted at Illinois State University hosts an open mic night on Saturdays and *Dare To Suck* is their core value, their rallying cry, and the basis on which they attract new talent. In their own words:

"Dare to Suck is not a lowering of the bar. It is a raising of the bar. It means trying something that is very likely outside your grasp, yet being willing to do it in front of an audience anyway."

– *Theatre of Ted*

Thanks Theatre of Ted. You kinda took the words right out of my mouth.

You could say I'm speechless. Again.

Got A *Dare To Suck* Story?

If you have a *Dare To Suck* story that sucks more than mine, send it to me. Our address and further details on how to connect are at the back of this book.

If it really sucks, I might feature you in a future book *Chicken Soup For The Sucker's Soul: Stories Of Leaders Who Have Turned Their Epic Screw-Ups Into Major Success Stories*. I bet we'd make Jack Canfield so very proud.

"It's a simple solution...you change one thing, and suddenly you've changed everything."

— REBECCA ONIE

#10

GIVE IT A NEW TWIST

People think innovation is this big scary thing but it's a lot more simple than you might think. While innovation can be a breakthrough, world-changing, invention that has never existed in people's imagination before...it can also be a simple twist on an old, tried-tested-and-true product.

A New Twist On An Old Product

During one of the brainstorming meetings at Ogilvy, a 26-year-old intern, held up one of the Shreddies, and joked, "It isn't a square, it's a diamond."

Viola! Diamond Shreddies was born — the same product, but with a revamped image.

The tone of the advertising campaign was humorous and ironic so consumers were well aware that the product was the same. Some of the commercials featured funny focus groups in which the product was tested and people stated rather curious things, such that Diamond Shreddies not only looked better, but tasted better than the original!

The website stated, "Recent advances in cereal technology have allowed us to take Shreddies cereal to a whole new level of geometric superiority." They even sold a "Combo Pack" that supposedly contained both versions.

The brand sold out four-months supply in two months and sales went up by 18%.[14]

The message was clear: Old is boring. New is EXCITING!...*and the ability to poke fun at yourself doesn't hurt either.*

Avocados anyone?

I love them but I'm probably not going to take pack one along with with a fork, knife, and napkin, so I can have a healthy snack in between meetings.

Cue: Avocado Innovation.

Convenience trumps for busy consumers, and as the popularity of avocados continues to rise, food companies are innovating with the goal of incorporating the ingredient into formats that are portable.

Avocado Chocolate anyone? Or what about dried avocado chips? Yes, please!

The lesson is simple: **Look for ways you can create a simple twist on something that is standard in your business** so that you can offer something new, fill a gap, and stand out in the marketplace.

Food For Thought...

Are you selling a product in a saturated niche?
Do you wonder why your sales aren't where they need to be?

Incremental innovation will help you lead change faster by making small adjustments to your existing product or product line, or marketing approach, to help create differentiation and improve your competitive positioning.

Here are three ideas for giving your current product or service a new twist:

1. Tap Into Consumer Emotions

The reason this is so powerful is that when we experience strong emotion, the brain activity in our prefrontal cortexes – the part of the brain that is in charge of executive function – shuts down. We're no longer in analysis mode. We're just absorbing it all. This means we're less anxious and more open to being influenced.

The Diamond Shreddies campaign successfully leveraged this by eliciting humor. Mars Inc. last year created a frightening short horror film series[15] during the Halloween season to promote its candy products, and Nescafe drove UK sales up by over 50%[16] when they ran a series of adverts featuring the Gold Blend couple that began a sizzling romance over a steaming cup of their advertised coffee.

2. Change The Context

When 3M developed an adhesive to stick on bulletin boards, the product never caught on. A chemist at the company, Arthur Fry, didn't give up and kept looking at the glue for new uses. One day, while singing in his church choir, he dropped his bookmark from his hymnbook. A lightbulb went off in his head as he realized the glue's primary function should be attaching the adhesive to paper rather than to a fixed surface. He could make notes on it and stick it to a page in his hymnbook in place of a bookmark and never lose his place.[17] By changing the context – bulletin board to paper – he gave the POST-IT new life.

3. Modify The Element

Adding chocolate to avocado allows it to be portable which makes it appealing for busy people on the go. It allows appeals to gourmet chocolate lovers that are on the lookout for a new taste.

Can you add or remove an ingredient? Add avocado spread to mini crackers. Wrap it up in new packaging and you've got a yummy snackable treat.

Can you change the structure? Grind up the avocado and turn it into a superfood that people can add to their smoothies.

Change the form? Remove the pit and the skin, cut them in half, and sell them frozen.

You get the idea...***Now, it's your turn.***

ACTION STEP

Write down your current challenge or a product you have that you'd like to improve upon – then use one of the following techniques to brainstorm ideas:

Tap Into Consumer Emotions

Can you use emotion to connect more deeply with your audience? What would happen if you stirred up anger? Fear? Love? Humor? Horror? Awe? Wonderment? Hope? Surprise?

Change The Context

Look at your product in a fresh way and find another use for it. Can you find a new use for an old idea, product, or service? Can you give it new context and new meaning?

Modify The Element

What can be modified? Can you add or remove an element?
Can you change the structure? The dimensions? The process?
Change the form? Magnify it? Make it smaller? Faster?

"As you start to walk out on the way, the way appears."

— RUMI

#11

WALK AND TALK

Apart from those individuals who are retired or semi-retired, and purposely spending less time in the office and more time on the golf course, I don't think I can think of a leader who isn't busy.

I mean insanely busy. I'm sure many of you reading this are no exception.

You know who you are. Every fifteen minutes in your calendar is accounted for – and any spare time is used to play catch up with the one hundred and one things on your checklist that are still outstanding. More often than not, you end up taking work home in the evenings and weekends just to stay on top of things.

Sooner or later, your productivity suffers. Your energy suffers. Your capacity to think clearly suffers. You can't seem to find the time to go to the gym. You're not fully present when when with your family. And with all those team lunches and customer dinners, your waistline has expanded while your creativity has nose-dived. True or true?!

81% of participants came up with more ideas while walking outside

A growing body of evidence suggests we think better when we walk. Researchers at Stanford University had people think up new uses for common objects while sitting at a desk, walking on a treadmill, walking outside, or bring rolled outside while in a wheelchair. They found that 81% of the participants came up with more ideas while walking outside than sitting indoors,[18] and the average creative output increased by 60%.[19]

Another study shows that people who walk have more creativity, greater focus, and a higher level of engagement than those that sit at their desk or in a boardroom.[20] (I call it a *bored-room* when leaders are twirling their pens, checking their phones and wondering when lunch is due but I digress..!)

Say "Hello" to Walking Meetings

A walking meeting is a meeting that takes places while you are out walking. It is a great opportunity to not only get the blood flowing, but it also **enhances three tools you must possess in abundance as a future-focused leader: creativity, innovation and communication.**

Steve Jobs was famous for taking walking meetings – especially when he was meeting people for the first time. Mark Zuckerberg has been known to take new potential hires on a hiking trail near Facebook's headquarters.[21] I personally love walking meetings and make it a habit of taking a walk whether I need to discuss something with a member of my team. And if I'm in a creative funk, a 'walk and talk' will quickly clear my head and spawn new ideas.

The act of walking – particularly outside – opens up the free flow of ideas - particularly when it comes to creative **divergent thinking.**

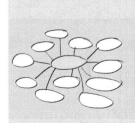

Divergent thinking is a thought process or method used to generate creative ideas by exploring many possible solutions.

Walking meetings improve divergent thinking leading to an average 60% increase in creative ideas.

Now you may be wondering...

Is it really worth the extra time and effort to go outside to discuss the development of your latest and greatest product? Will taking a new hire in the outdoors vs interviewing them at your desk make THAT much of a difference?

Six Advantages to Incorporating Walking Meetings Into Your Schedule

1.   **A Walking Meeting is more personal**. Often, it's just you and one other person or two at the most. You get to connect more than if you are in a large group where some people barely get their voice heard. Connection builds trust, which creates a free flow of ideas.

2. **Walking Meetings don't involve a desk, stuffy room, a laptop, or notepad**. These potentials limitations and barriers to communication and creativity are removed right off the bat leaving you open to fresh inspiration and insight.

3. **Walking Meetings allow you to let off steam and bring presence and clarity to fuzzy minds.** The physical activity of walking generates increased blood flow and oxygen to the brain which enhances cognition.

4. **Walking Meetings lead to fresh creative ideas**, and thus boost productivity during informal brainstorming sessions.

5. **Walking Meetings enable you to think on your feet** (literally) and problem-solve where otherwise you may not see alternatives.

6. **Walking Meetings level the playing field**. Walking side by sides makes the environment less formal and the conversation more authentic, more personal, and more honest.

When NOT To Walk and Talk

When you need to tap into ***convergent thinking***, i.e. you want to reach consensus and find the single best solution to a problem instead of many different possibilities.

Convergent Thinking is a problem solving technique in which ideas from different fields or participants are brought together to find a single optimum solution to a clearly defined problem.

These are the times you want to be sitting down.

ACTION STEP

It's Game Time...

Are you sitting down right now? We're going to play a quick game called *Remote Associates*. If you are sitting down, the odds of you getting the right answer in this game will increase significantly, so go ahead and take a seat for a minute if you are able to. We're going to test this theory out on you right now.

Are you ready? Here we go...

Think of the one word that forms a common pairing with the three words below:

Gap

Door

Sign

Take your time and don't read on until you have at least considered the answer. Just let your eyes lift up off the page while you ponder.

Come back here and continue reading when you're ready.

~~~~~

Do you know what it is?

The correct answer is *Stop*. Stop Gap, Door Stop, Stop Sign.

Most people will perform significantly worse on this convergent task and will be less likely to come up with the correct answer while walking than sitting. Test it out on a friend or colleague and see!

Know Which To Use When

Your end goal will determine the means. Understanding the distinction between convergent and divergent thinking will help you to determine whether taking a walking meeting or sitting in the boardroom is the better solution.

If your end goal is to develop out-of-the-box ideas, then a walking meeting is the preferred choice. However, if getting consensus and coming to a decision or solution is your desired outcome, a traditional meeting around the conference room table is going to be your best setting.

And while a walking meeting might be more difficult in locations where privacy is a factor (think New York and Washington D.C.) or the city just isn't set up for walking (Los Angeles comes to mind here) get creative. For those determined enough to capitalize on this strategy, I trust you will find a way.

"Out beyond ideas of wrongdoing And rightdoing there is a field. I'll meet you there."

— RUMI

#12

THINK THE UNTHINKABLE

In 1900, in a feature entitled *What May Happen In The Next Hundred Years*[22] in The Ladies Home Journal, an American civil engineer called John Elfreth Watkins predicted the state of the world in the year 2000.

He proclaimed: "Express trains [will run at] one hundred and fifty miles per hour."

In the year 2000, Amtrak's flagship high-speed rail line, the Acela Express, opened between Boston and Washington, DC. It has the capability to reach top speeds of 150mph.

He proclaimed: "Man will see around the world. Persons and things of all kinds will be brought within focus of cameras connected electrically with screens at opposite ends of circuits, thousands of miles at a span."

Today, we call this television.

And he proclaimed: "Photographs will be telegraphed from any distance. If there be a battle in China a hundred years hence, snapshots of its most striking events will be published in the newspapers an hour later...photographs will reproduce all of nature's colours."

Talk about an eerily accurate prediction of how we have come to utilize digital color photography as well as the speed of transmission of global news today!

At that time, his critics thought him outrageous.
Today, he is hailed a genius.

While there are companies out there that are already committed to creating a culture of innovation, how many of these leaders are really comfortable when people enter the *Zone of Outrageousness?*

Zone of Outrageousness:

mental territory that is so daring, defiant, and radical, it is unthinkable.

Where Alan Greenspan stumbled...

Why did Alan Greenspan, economist and former Federal Reserve chairman – once considered to be the infallible rockstar of the U.S. economy with 40+ years of experience on his resume – confess to Congress after the housing bubble in 2006 that he had 'found a flaw' in free market theory?

When he was pressed by a congressman who asked whether his view of the world, his ideology, was not working, Greenspan replied:

> *"Absolutely. Precisely. You know that's precisely the reason I was shocked. Because I have been going for forty years or more with very considerable evidence that it was working exceptionally well."*[23]

Had Greenspan dared to enter the *Zone of Outrageousness* – the unthinkable notion that banks *might* not do a stellar job in self-regulating and *could* end up lending to unfit borrowers, and, therefore, *should* be monitored by external regulators, **he might have acted differently and perhaps averted the 2007 subprime mortgage financial crisis.**

In The Zone: Elon Musk

When Elon Musk created the first viable production electric car of the modern era (Tesla Roadster), co-founded the world's largest Internet payment system (PayPal) and designed a private successor to the Space Shuttle (F9/Dragon), he was declaring to the world that he was only interested in opportunities within industries that people deemed impossible, difficult, or out of reach.

On how to heat Mars to sustain humankind, critics called him outrageous[24] for responding: "The fast way is to drop thermonuclear weapons over the poles."

In The Zone: A Corning Scientist

During a planning meeting at Corning Inc., one of their leading scientists asked a question that threatened Corning's core capability: What would happen if a competitor found a way to deposit magnetic film on glass *without* high temperatures?[25]

Colleagues laughed and poked fun at him but graced him with the space to think the unthinkable. Ultimately, this sparked an impromptu discussion about temperature range, new outcomes that might arise, and the kind of resources that would be needed to address such a scenario.

When we challenge the status quo in our organizations and colleagues stay present enough with our ideas to explore them...that's where the magic happens.

If our ideas are so outlandish they place us squarely in the *Zone of Outrageousness*, speak up anyway. Critics a hundred years from today may just hail you as the John Watkins of the 21st century.

At the time that John Elfreth Watkins forecasted the role digital color photography would play in the media, black and white photography was still a marvel, color photographs were in their infancy, and it would have taken a week for a story in China to be reported in a Western newspaper.

John Elfreth Watkins didn't get it all right...and neither will you. Watkins predicted that in the year 2000, everybody will walk ten miles a day. With breakthroughs in transport over the last century, he missed the mark in this – as well as other – arenas.

But there's hope still...

In the year 2022, after twenty million leaders have read this book and are actively practicing the *Walk and Talk* principle, people might just look back and proclaim, *"That Watkins was a genius for predicting that one right, too..."*

[See what I did here?...I'm *Thinking The Unthinkable*.]

Live Your Creed

Many of today's companies bleat "There is no such thing as a bad idea" like the animals on George Orwell's farm bleated "Four legs good, two legs baa-d". The chant becomes meaningless over time and serves no purpose other than to drown out minority opinion.

When leaders don't give their people permission to think the unthinkable, new ideas quickly get suppressed. While many intellectually understand that thinking differently during times of change is critical, you can tell the mantra isn't being lived the moment one brave person comes up with something remotely fantastical, unconventional, freakish, or impractical that has never been conceived of before, and a cynic responds by shutting the minority opinion down.

ACTION STEP

To encourage thinking the unthinkable, three things need to happen:

1. **Nurture this capability within you.** You won't always be on point – but it might spark an idea that another person will latch on to – leading to a chain of events that sparks an unforeseen shift in humanity. Giving yourself and team members space to think the unthinkable stretches everyone to consider what other possibilities might exist.

2. **Be on the alert for inadvertently shutting other people down.** When others around you think the unthinkable, you may not realize you are demonstrating your disapproval by unconsciously snickering at them. You may not realize you are cutting them off mid-sentence. You may not realize you have waived your hand dismissively at them – as if the train of thought is unworthy of further consideration. Be on the alert for such behaviors.

3. **Discuss what is unmentionable.** Yale University's Woodward Report advocates the need for its students to be free to "think the unthinkable,

discuss the unmentionable, and challenge the unchallengeable".[26] It also calls for tolerating "the provocative, the disturbing, and the unorthodox".

When you encounter people who think differently to you or people who have entered the *Zone of Outrageousness*, it will rock your core belief system and possibly threaten your entire identity.

While I challenge you to boldly fling (or gently nudge) open the edges of your comfort zone to embrace new paradigms and turn old ones on their head, I also encourage you to meet people where they are at and have the courageous conversations that foster understanding and respect for people, wherever they are on the journey.

Withhold the need to pass judgment. Move at your own pace while recognizing that others are moving at theirs.

"We must learn that doing good is good for business."

— SIR RICHARD BRANSON

#13

DO MORE GOOD

The tsunami of events over the past few years have tested businesses in unprecedented ways. The #MeToo Movement, the immigration ban, the transgender military ban, the decision to withdraw from the Paris agreement, the UK's wavering around Brexit, the influx of natural global disasters...all these events, and more, have forced organizations to react.

Many CEOs have utilized their voice and influence to issue public statements letting their stance be known. This means that doing your part in promoting social responsibility and good governance is paramount if you want to stand a better chance of succeeding in today's economy. Passively sitting by the sidelines and responding to change when legislation demands it, or taking the *Would be nice if we can fit it in stance* is no longer acceptable.

It is no longer enough to have a winning product line and be a market leader in your space. As a leader, you are expected to look at the gender and cultural balance of your executive team, your boards, and your individual business units. You are expected to give a voice to the people that serve you – no matter their age, cultural background, physical ability, sexual orientation, or background.

In today's global marketplace, the onus is landing firmly on corporate decision makers to address and advance global and social challenges...and indeed, any issue that matters to their individual contributors, customers, or the community.

With globalization in full force and the population becoming more diverse, companies are expected to create products and experiences that embrace this wide spectrum of perspectives. Whether you realize it or not, as a leader, all eyes are on you as the people within your circle of influence want to know what you stand for, and what you are proactively doing for the benefit of their cause and society at large.

Today's generation are mission-driven and purpose-driven. They care less about a paycheck or the cost of an item, than they care that you are doing the right thing by them and others.

Nearly 60% of employees who are proud of their company's social responsibility are engaged at their jobs and 55% of consumers are willing to pay more for products from socially responsible companies[27].

- **Nearly 60%** of employees who are proud of their company's social responsibility are engaged at their jobs.

- **55%** of consumers are willing to pay more for products from socially-responsible companies.

The demand for more conscious businesses and for sustainable products and services is clear, and so the question remains: *How are you reacting?*

Many big businesses are actively seeking out suppliers and partners who are not only driven by profit, but can also demonstrate that they care about people and the planet. **Are you?**

Craig's Story

When Haiti was struck by a devastating earthquake in 2010, UPS responded by delivering food and other resources to the site. One of its managers, Craig Arnold, found another way to make a difference.

Craig had heard reports of fraud. Aid workers had set up a system where more than 10,000 victims could get access to food, medicine, and hygiene supplies. However, the system was flawed; it consisted simply of paper index cards with the handwritten names of the eligible families. People would arrive at the front of the line after hours of waiting, only to find out that their allocated supply had already been taken. Others, claiming to be them, had already taken their supplies, perhaps with the view of selling them on the black market.

With supplies short, Craig and some colleagues at UPS put together an automated system using just a laptop, identity cards with bar-codes, and the already-built company proprietary tool – the UPS Trackpad. Within a week, the team had virtually eliminated the possibility of theft and reduced the chaos and stress that had built up in the waiting lines with his simple low-tech solution: to issue every eligible family with an identity card.

Craig Arnold's solution cost UPS a few thousand dollars, but had as great an impact as any seven-figure contributions made to relief organizations in Haiti.

"We don't have the resources."

Many leaders I talk with struggle with looking beyond what is good for their companies – especially if they don't feel they have the resources to respond to the changes that are happening, or support the many causes that are crying out for their attention.

However, you can make an impact at whatever scale you are able to. Employees intuitively know when their leaders are putting their best foot forward and are genuinely committed to bettering the local and global communities, and will follow suit. If your efforts are sincere, then no matter the size or reach, it will result in improved output. Every effort, big or small, will result in a win, as employees are more likely to be productive and creative when working for companies they believe in and can stand behind.

In UPS' case, Craig Arnold took the initiative on a small project that created a big win. It worked because he utilized the exact steps we teach socially conscious leaders:

He chose his focus: He kept his eyes open to where help was needed.

He leveraged his company's assets: He looked at what resources his company already had in place, and with a few thousand dollars, a bold idea, a few colleagues with specialized knowledge, and some business acumen, he was able to design a solution that made a dramatic positive impact on the relief efforts in Haiti and other disaster sites that utilized the technology later.

He built upon the success of others: Arnold's initiative worked because he was building on the infrastructure that The Salvation Army already had in place. The strategic partnership helped families in need, saved lives, built goodwill, and much, much, more.

One point worth noting: Craig Arnold was a manager. He wasn't a C-Suite Executive. He wasn't a VP – at least not at the time this happened. (Today he is). Oftentimes, we mistakenly think that leading change is up to the senior leadership team or key decision makers. Craig's story shows how **one person who takes initiative can be a force of good, no matter the role, title, or level of responsibility held.**

ACTION STEP

THE 1-2-3 SOCIAL RESPONSIBILITY STRATEGY:

1.   *CHOOSE Your Focus*

Keep your eyes and ears open for what is going on in your local community, your region, your country, and the other side of the world. Or pick a cause you care deeply about – gender equality, human rights, climate change, transparency – these are all areas where you can make an impact.

2.   *LEVERAGE Your Assets*

Know what your strengths are and what infrastructure and resources you already have in place. Unless you have deep pockets, this is not the time to reinvent the wheel but to leverage what you already do well.

3.   *BUILD Upon The Success Of Others*

Put your focus on where there is already momentum and where your company's additional efforts, or your existing operations and initiatives, could make a significant difference for others who are already leading change in your chosen arena.

RAMP IT UP

Here are 3 additional ideas for **amplifying** your good deeds:

Partner with Non-Profits

- Give non-profits monetary donations as well as provide them with access to leading-edge training that helps them achieve their goals.
- Volunteer your time (and encourage team members and employees to volunteer also).
- Offer in-kind donations of your products or services.

Increase Your Media Coverage

- Reach out to media outlets to cover your story. The bigger and better the benefits to others, the better the media coverage will be.

Offer Gift-Matching Programs

- Double the impact you make on your chosen non-profit's fundraising efforts by matching the donations that your employees give, dollar for dollar.

At the end of the day, taking care of others is simply the right thing to do, but for businesses to extend their impact, it helps to have added incentives and a dedicated support structure. **Schedule** a time to talk with me about additional win-win strategies, or to partner with us in developing a robust Corporate Social Responsibility program in your organization.

"Understanding the nuances of rivalry can help extend your career. It doesn't mean you'll be holding hands across the finish line. It means their presence makes you better, faster, stronger. Because of them, you'll find out exactly what you are made of."

– LEENA PATEL

#14

TEAM UP WITH YOUR RIVALS

What do the following organizations have in common?

Coke and Pepsi
McDonald's and Burger King
Starbucks and Dunkin' Donuts
Fedex and UPS
Boeing and Airbus

You guessed it! They are rivals. In fact, they are some of the biggest rivals in recent history.

In any high-performing environment, rivalry is inevitable. Vigorous rivalry serves companies well, but it can also bring out the worst in people.

When I was in my early twenties, I got fired (the firm called it "non-renewal of a contract") because a jealous colleague told my then boss "I don't think Leena is happy here. She wants to move to the US."

This was in the nineties, when I lived in London, England, and was a soloist in one of the country's leading dance companies.

*Wow...*I thought to myself, reading the formal letter they had sent me in the mail in disbelief. *I told her it was a dream I'd like to fulfill five years from now! I never said anything about not being happy in this role. I love my job! Talk about taking information shared in casual locker-room conversation, twisting it around, and using it to stab me in the back.*

Little did I know then, the blessing in disguise this expression of rivalry would turn out to be. It led to me retiring from the stage, moving to Canada, and playing a behind-the-scenes role, coaching and consulting for world-class athletes and performers including Jaime King, Celine Dion, and the artistes of Cirque du Soleil. These experiences catapulted me onto the path I am on today – channeling my creativity and business acumen to help companies grow through strategic innovation. I have to thank an early rival for that.

The Power of Strategic Collaboration

When you expend resources over things that hold little value – like weakening your competition or preventing them from getting a bigger piece of the pie, you have less energy, time, and money available to *solve the actual problem that needs to be solved*. The best case outcome is a decline in profitability; the worst case is being wiped out of the market as the more nimble, smaller, companies swoop in to take advantage of your negligence.

Oftentimes, strategic collaboration can offer an immediate payoff for everyone by enabling organizations to pool resources and reduce costs.

Visa and Mastercard Did It...

During the sixties and seventies, banks worked together to launch Visa and Mastercard on a global level, reaping the efficiency benefits of a centralized payment system, lower marketing costs, and increased brand recognition.

Amazon and Best Buy Did It...

In 2018, rivals Amazon and Best Buy partnered up to sell Amazon's Fire TV Edition smart TVs. Best Buy became the exclusive retailer and in exchange for opening up Amazon's technology to a wider array of shoppers, the partnership allowed Best Buy to tap into Amazon's huge customer network.

BBC and ITV Did It...

In 2019, UK television rivals, BBC and ITV announced plans to create a streaming service called BritBox to be launched later in the year - with the goal of confronting heavy competition from Netflix.

...*Even The Birds and The Bees Do It!*

Whether you compete against your rival directly, you team up to amplify your impact in areas that your customers value, or you follow their success from a distance, your opponent's accomplishments can be valuable fuel that drives your own success.

While teaming up with your rival(s) is not always going to be the best solution in all scenarios, know that if you *do* decide to explore the notion further, there is a right way and a wrong way to enter a partnership with a competitor. If it brings up some resistance in you, probe deeper into your own situation so that you can make a more conscious, level-headed decision.

The Bottom Line: By taking a renewed look at your competition/collaboration ratio and shifting the balance towards becoming customer/supplier centric, you will **open the door to more enlightened business partnerships.**

ACTION STEP

Chances are you have at least one rival: whether it's a peer you are looking to outperform, someone with an eye on the same promotion, or your nemesis at your company's biggest competitor.

Questions To Ask Yourself:

- Who are your biggest rivals at work, and what specifically do you admire most about them? Hint: If you can't think of anyone, ask yourself who you constantly compare yourself to.
- Has this person's performance ever motivated you to think differently, or work harder or smarter?
- What big goals could you accomplish by teaming up with each other?
- How can you foster mutual respect and keep the rivalry friendly and healthy, rather than bitter and destructive?

Keep your rivals close – and connect with them often. **You'll find that you'll be more creative, more focused, more visionary, and more determined when they are around.**

Now, bring on the healthy competition.

"Here we are, unique, eternal aspects of consciousness with an infinity of potential, and we have allowed ourselves to become an unthinking, unquestioning blob of conformity and uniformity. A herd. Once we concede to the herd mentality, we can be controlled and directed by a tiny few. And we are."

— DAVID ICKE

#15

MINIMIZE GROUPTHINK

Consider a typical day in your current role at work. How much time do you spend in meetings, responding to e-mails, or talking to colleagues on the phone? If you're like most, this number totals around 80% on a daily basis, leaving you little time for all the important work you need to complete on your own.

There has been an influx of studies done in recent years showing that people working in teams tend to innovate faster, see mistakes more quickly, and find better solutions to problems. In a 2015 study,[27] executives said that profitability increases when workers are persuaded to collaborate more. Makes sense, right? After all, most people enjoy – and even welcome – a bit of camaraderie with colleagues while navigating the stresses of day to day challenges.

The problem is that this pattern has created a habit and leads leaders to rely on collaboration more and more to solve their company problems. As business becomes increasingly global and complex, leaders have been viewing teamwork as fundamental to their organizations and key to breaking down silo mentality and creating organizational success. And indeed it can be.

However, let's pause to note that over the past twenty years, managers and employees are increasing time spent in collaborative activities by 50% or more.[28]

Take a moment to digest that more fully –

"Over the past twenty years, managers and employees are increasing time spent in collaborative activities by 50% or more."[28]

What began as a powerful productivity strategy has now become an organizational bottleneck: Work doesn't progress until Joe, John, Joanie, Jennifer, Jerry, Jack, AND Jill have given their input.

Traditional funding agencies have pushed startups in this direction as well. By placing high value on having bigger and bigger teams, they are mistakenly buying into the fallacy that larger teams equate to higher quality output. As these bootstrapping smaller companies have grown and scaled up over the years, they have maintained this leadership habit.

BIG MYTH:
Larger Teams = Higher Quality Output

The reality is there is a tipping point after which the advantages of bigger teams begin to decline. As team size grows, disruptiveness declines. Indeed, it appears that when it comes to putting an innovation-driven team together:

SIZE MATTERS!

Big research teams tend to work on existing theories rather than instigating new ones. They are more likely to produce high-impact papers that boast a high number of citations. And while building upon an existing theory is an important research endeavor, this will rarely shift paradigms. In contrast, the most disruptive papers, scientific findings, software products and patents tend to be produced by small groups, highlighting the value in small team collaborations.

As team size grows, disruptiveness declines.

Suzy's Story

During her time as CEO of digital agency Moxie, Suzy Deering witnessed layers of bureaucracy hindering progress internally. She decided to restructure her teams as smaller units so they could be more responsive to their clients' needs.

After the pivot, one unit fluidly tapped into what was actually going on in one of its client's restaurants. The unit came up with the idea of a pop-up which allowed in-the-moment dialogue with restaurant goers about their love for Chick-fil-A and cows – and then drove engagement by retweeting customer quotes in a creative and visual way.

Having smaller teams eliminates the layers of bureaucracy that hinder progress.

Groupthink:

a psychological phenomenon that occurs within a group of people in which the desire for conformity and consensus gives rise to engaging in thinking or decision-making practices that discourage creativity or individual responsibility.

To minimize Groupthink, start by looking at how you form teams.

Pop Quiz Time!

You have a group of thirty people and two teams need to be formed.

Do you:

    A. Divvy everyone up randomly into two groups of fifteen.

    B. Divide them up using some kind of classification (for example, gender, technical versus non-technical, experienced versus newbies).

    C. Other?

Did it occur to you to create two groups of two in order to create smaller group sizes? It may not always be practical or feasible – *but did it even cross your mind?*

So what's an optimum team size, Leena?

Unfortunately, there is no absolute answer to this as it depends on the task at hand and the skillset of the group. If you are putting together a team of cleaners to clean a 30,000 sq. ft. office complex, there is no doubt that a team of thirty will clean faster than a team of five. However, **for tasks that require idea generation, strategic analysis, thought leadership, or out of the box insights, banish big teams.**

In my firm, because we are in the business of constantly pushing the boundaries and thinking differently, both within our business and for our clients, five is the magic number we have as our current maximum. After that, we often split into sub-teams to ensure that everyone gets a chance to speak and be heard, and the team doesn't get stuck into Groupthink mode.

ACTION STEP

Figure out your magic number(s)

While teams *can* be effective with six, seven, eight, or even nine members, pay close attention to their output and be on the alert for *social loafing* (diminished individual effort) with these higher numbers.

Ultimately, if you want to push the limits of what's possible while having an insurance policy against a future that is unknown, unpredictable, or uncertain, you must combine both: utilize big teams to develop and solidify existing ideas while championing small teams to work on the higher-risk, higher-reward initiatives.

Just ensure you banish those big teams in areas you want to make quantum leap discoveries or demonstrate game-changing thought leadership.

"When you are saying 'yes' to others, make sure are not saying 'no' to yourself."

— PAULO COELHO

#16

SAY NO TO GREAT IDEAS

With the presence of many competitors vying for the attention of hungry buyers, the marketplace is filled with noise. Gurus, advisors, board members, and others will suggest you hire more salespeople, spend more in marketing, lower your prices to remain competitive. As you grow more successful and your company gets bigger, you will be bombarded with requests for media interviews, partnership offers, and more. Everyone and his uncle will be there to give you advice, and dangle juicy carrots and shiny objects in front of you. Some of them will be really good and you will be tempted.

Your sole responsibility as a leader is to obliterate all noise; focus on no more than three things and be relentless in saying no to everything else.

Celine's Story

In my early days consulting for Celine Dion in the late nineties, I was in the Toronto office of her then Chief Marketing Officer, Dave Platel, on an almost weekly basis. Each time, there would be an astronomical amount of mail piled up on his desk that had poured in from media, fans, non-profits, songwriters, foundations...and the like. Each of them asked for some kind of request from Celine. *Could she perform at X? Could she donate to Y? Could she partner with Z?*

Dave and the management team would said say no to 99% of these requests. While many of these were great ideas, worthy proposals, and amazing platforms, they simply didn't have the capacity to say YES to them all.

I recall being in a car with him on a day when he had a couple of bags of CDs that songwriters had sent for Celine's consideration in the trunk. To make use of the drive time, we played as many songs as we could. Many were great songs but not quite the right fit for Celine's style and voice. Once in a while, we'd come across one that would blow us away, and we'd hit play and re-listen with more intent. We could absolutely imagine *someone* singing that song, we'd say. At the end of the day, it just didn't end up being Celine.

Celine and her late husband-manager, Rene, had a vision for the direction they wanted to take each album and maintaining a laser sharp focus enabled her team to deliver in excellence to her audiences and partners. This ability to obliterate all noise and frequently say no to even the great ideas has enabled her to focus on continuously break new ground instead of following the herd. It has also kept her an industry leader decades later.

Tim's Story

Apple's current Chief Executive Officer, Tim Cook, too, has kept this philosophy front and center. He has no qualms with rejecting good ideas on a daily basis.

We say no to great ideas in order to keep the amount of things we focus on very small in number, so that we can put enormous energy behind the ones we do choose, so that we can deliver the best products in the world.[29]

— Tim Cook

This philosophy has been anchored in the company since the time Steve Jobs came back to Apple; he stripped down the product line and focused on increasing the quality of the products that remained. Jobs and Cook have succeeded in leading the company through times of change by obliterating all noise, saying NO to even the great ideas, and keeping their main thing their main thing.

You must do the same.

My Story

Before I started speaking to large audiences I didn't know the level of skill required to deliver at a world class level. I had no idea that having a process in place *before I got on stage* was the key to audiences getting exactly what they wanted and needed. I had no idea of the nuances involved in telling impactful stories that stuck in the audience's mind long after the event, and I had no idea how to continue to add value to the client above and beyond what they had paid for *after* delivering my keynote.

Once I identified those skills as necessary for our long-term success, I obsessively worked to develop them. I sat with my team and mapped out a game plan and identified what we needed to do achieve our targets and the role each of us played in this.

Today, we don't run Facebook ads. We don't hire lead generation experts to pitch C-Suite executives and VPs for us. We don't spend time and money creating fancy brochures and writing out proposals.

I go out and speak. That's how I connect with my audience. I've built this business by mastering a craft and adding massive value and my team understands this and are on board with it. It's our #1 marketing strategy and it works.

Now when I speak at conferences and events around the world, I consistently get ratings in the 95-100%. I have been ranked by a leading speaking organization as one of the top 5% of speakers in the world and declared "the world's best female speaker"[30] by peers.

While I am still continuously looking to up my game, I never take this feedback for granted. When event managers tell me I understood their audience and provided more value than any other speaker they had previously hired, I know it is because I have worked tirelessly over the last seven years to master this craft so that clients get an outstanding experience. And I know that I have been able to do this because I have obliterated the noise and said NO to many other great marketing ideas.

ACTION STEP

Obliterate noise by answering the following three questions:

1. What are the three major needle-moving objectives that you want to accomplish?
2. What key strategies do you have to put into place to meet them?
3. What skills do you need to develop or what hurdles do you need to overcome to accomplish them?

A Word of Warning

While it's important to maintain focus on your key objectives, be clear about which are NOT your major moves, so that you know what distractions to avoid.

A mistake many company leaders make in their efforts to grow bigger is that their focus broadens as they start paying attention to the noise and adding this and that.

Get more skilled at saying no. Your success as a leader is in direct proportion to your ability to stay focused on your objective. Your only objective is to identify your key objectives and then strategically align yourself to achieve each of them.

Increase The Output That Matters.
The rest... is NOISE.

Need Help In Deciding What Objectives To Focus On?

I run half-day and full-day strategy days with my clients where I sit and (1) help you figure out all the components that are involved in accurately answering this question as it pertains to your business and (2) map out a strategic game plan.

External support is invaluable in ensuring you have a fresh pair of eyes on your situation. Great consultants will **ensure you have the right ladder up against the right wall saving you both time and money.**

Let's connect.

"...put your feet in the right place, then stand firm."

— ABRAHAM LINCOLN

#17

AWAKEN THE NEW POWER

This happened in the recent past...

- **2018**. **Employees at Google** in New York City, Silicon Valley, Seattle, Hyderabad, London, Berlin, Zurich and other cities around the world protested the tech giant's handling of the sexual harassment cases against two male executives: they were awarded $105M in exit packages.

- **2018**. **A young student** spoke out about gun control. Emma Gonzalez bravely addressed a gun control rally in Florida, days after a gunman entered her school and killed 17 people and severely injured many more.

- **2019**. **19 black employees** at a UPS plant in Ohio have been subjected to racial harassment and discrimination from white co-workers. They filed a lawsuit which included allegations of being passed over for promotions, use of the N-word, and being ridiculed because of their race. Just two years prior, one employee, Antonio Lino, walked into work one morning to find two 13-knot nooses at his workstation. He took a photo and sent it to corporate who dismissed it as a joke and told him to delete it. Instead, the employee posted the evidence on social media and took it to the Ohio Civil Rights Commission.[31]

Whatever your political beliefs, your ideas on gun control, or your perspective on diversity, equity, and inclusion, I give these examples because they represent boldness from individuals who are not in traditional positions of power, in a world where we have witnessed and experienced much inhumanity and injustice.

Consider the direction our world is going. The leaders in industry are leaving behind them a massive wake of nothing. Many are in the crest of their careers and within the next two decades they will be looking for their exit strategies. That leaves who on the bench?

Us.

There's a gap. And we must fill the gap. We will be the new leaders. And we've got to be prepared to step into their shoes and take business and technology and education and politics forward.

The NEW Power

Over the last few decades, people in various circles have called it speaking truth to power. But this is the NEW power. Because of the rise of social media and the influence we have as a collective to lead change, **the power has shifted from the individual, and is swiftly moving into the hands of the masses.**

That includes you and me, baby.

For those of you who are wondering what awakening the new power has to do with raising your innovation IQ, here it is:

Bold ideas and inventions only emerge in an environment where people are free to speak up.
And speaking up and awakening the new power is not limited to supporting your organization in creating new products or services, or improving upon existing ones, it is about innovating on the standards, rules, and modes of behavior we once perceived as 'normal' in the

workplace – but that no longer serve us as individuals, as leaders, as businesses, and as a human race.

The problem...

The tragedy is that not many people feel equipped to step into this level of conscious leadership today. The workplace doesn't adequately train us. Education doesn't adequately prepare us. This is the #1 reason I ventured into disrupting the business world – because I want to empower influencers to lead with more skill and more heart. Quite simply, the old way is no longer working anymore.

There are some people in the world who are doing things that are unethical – whether in business, on the global political stage, or within our homes or communities – who don't have our best interests at heart and are not listening to what we want. They are not standing behind their business and we've got to speak up.

But we don't always, do we?

How many times have you caught yourself (or heard someone else) saying:

- *(S)he's the boss. It's out of my control.*

- *I'm just doing my job. I don't want to get fired...*

- What can I do? I'm one small insignificant person...

I get that the fear of losing your job is a reality for many people...but allow me to offer some perspective: Groups in previous generations such as the abolitionists, the suffragettes, the leaders of the civil rights movements, and countless others stood up to power when faced with injustice so that we could live with the freedom we have today. They lived under much harsher times than most of us will ever experience.

At what point will we stop turning a blind eye and decide enough is enough?

Today's workforce, and the young generations that are following have a different standard for what they should live by. They are cause-driven and care deeply about making a difference. They are also incredibly loyal – but not loyal in a quiet, subservient way. They are loyal to the highest values of truth and non-violence. This generation has fire and dynamism, and they have every right to care deeply and to speak boldly because this is their time. This is the world they are inheriting...the world that Generation X's like myself, and the Baby Boomers who came before me, have created and are handing to them.

Young people have every right to say *not on my watch* – and my question is *why aren't we also*? Why are we so comfortable to sit back passively and believe we can't create change if we are not in a position of power? It just takes one candle to light a room...and one candle to light a thousand more. *What's holding us back?*

> **It just takes one candle to light a room...and one candle to light a thousand more.**

I believe there is a big difference between us saying *Oh yeah...that incident that happened the other day. Isn't that terrible?* And *What action can I take to prevent a situation like this happening again?*

Google employees protested – and the leadership team paid attention. Emma Gonzales spoke up – and CNN paid attention. Antonio Lino, along with nineteen other colleagues, spoke up – and now UPS is paying attention.

And now I challenge you...where are you not speaking up in your life? If you don't think the marketing strategy for your new product line is being inclusive, are you saying anything? If not, why not?

If your boss or the company you work for is not doing things in alignment with your values and beliefs, how can you make your voice be heard? How will you speak truth to power? And how will you awaken the new power so that the voice of the collective is louder than the voice of those who are leading us into the lion's den?

You wouldn't hesitate to say no to your child if you thought it was for the best and highest good. So why aren't we exhibiting that same courage of conviction in the community and at work? Why aren't we speaking out with more boldness?

I was interviewed on Fox News after a gunman opened fire on a crowd of concertgoers on the Las Vegas Strip in Nevada. Just before I went on air, I was told not to mention gun control. They wanted media guests to stay neutral and steered the interview away from questions that might lead me to take a political stance. I obliged, and yet in the wake of recent events, I wonder: *If the news channels provided a vehicle for more constructive dialogue that can raise public awareness, could incidents like this have been avoided?*

This same pattern is reflected in social media, too. I see people who are afraid to speak up or comment on challenging topics where there are no easy answers.

Afraid someone will unfriend them for sharing anything other than a neutral opinion. Those who do speak up, often hate on the people who hold an opposing perspective and don't provide the space to allow a dialogue to take place.

I applaud the brave men and women in the workplace who are out there and standing up, showing up, and speaking up without fear, or probably more accurately, speaking *despite* their fear.

I applaud these brave men and women for prioritizing doing the right thing versus the senseless thing. None of our colleagues, classmates, or neighbors, near or far, deserve to be on the receiving end of the actions of individuals or groups that threaten our identity, our safety, our right to speak up and be heard.

I applaud these brave men and women for daring to believe their voice and their opinion matters. Because of their faith in themselves and us, the workplace (and the world) is changing at an unprecedented pace. It is spurring innovations in corporate culture. It is spurring innovations in new product lines that are speaking to demographics that have long been ignored. The growth potential is huge for those paying attention and not threatened by the tidal wave.

And the awakening of this new power is inspiring millions to take the words and actions of a growing collective of brave souls to heart. It is giving them permission to be courageous also.

This is the brave new world we need to be embodying more deeply. Those who are speaking out and standing for something have my deepest respect and admiration for daring greatly. It's now time for each of us to awaken to this new power, build on the foundation of the brave individuals who have walked before us, and lead with courage. **Now is the time – and title or no title –** *you are a leader.*

A Lesson From Gandhi

I remember a story my Grandfather told me about Gandhi that speaks volumes about Gandhi's character. General Smuts, the South African Prime Minister who was on the receiving end of Gandhi's non-violent campaign, confessed to Gandhi that he could deal with railway employees who were angry and hateful and said he did not mind using crushing violence against them. However, he said, he had a hard time dealing violently with Gandhi because although the Mahatma opposed his policies of discrimination, he always treated him with respect and consideration. During World War II when the British Government, led by Sir Winston Churchill, unleashed a campaign against Gandhi, General Smuts refused to side with Churchill in saying anything bad about Gandhi.

Gandhi is proof it is possible to challenge others who hold different opinions to us, even when they are in a position of authority. His actions teach us to maintain respect for those we oppose by taking a stand against the action, not the person.

ACTION STEP

Ask Yourself:

- Why are you not exhibiting the same courage of conviction in the work and in the community as you would do with your loved ones?

- When opposing an injustice in the workplace (or elsewhere), are you able to separate the action from the person?

- How much is that inability to speak truth to your leaders in the workplace affecting your health, your relationships, your home life?

HOW TO AWAKEN THE NEW POWER

- **Be fearless in sharing your truth.** Strip away the layers of pretenses, embellishment, rationalization, minimization, and omission that are used as a matter of convenience in order to avoid confronting what needs to be brought out into the open. Even though it may be hurtful in the short term, we want the truth from others and others want it from us. Speaking your truth supports and

- inspires those around us to act from within them as well.

- **Stop turning a blind eye** to the problems in the workplace because you are not directly affected by them or because you think change is beyond your reach. Skepticism is just an excuse for not helping and speaking up for a cause you believe in. Stand for *something*.

- And while you stand, **stand against the action, not the person**. Use the new power of the collective voice to effect change where it matters. We owe it to ourselves. We owe it to our kids who are inheriting the world we have created. We owe it to the everyday folks who fill our history books, the folks who walked the hard path and stood up to power when faced with injustice so that we could live with the freedom we have today.

- **Let go of your need for approval from others.** We often turn to others for advice more frequently than we listen within, however, talking to others does not absolve you of the responsibility of heeding *your* truth. Anything anyone says to you is more often about themselves than it is about you. Therefore, in the final moment, be guided by your conscience. Stop living your life according to other people's truths or their definition of your truth. We can only surrender to the truth as we see it and we are ultimately responsible for the choices that we make. Do not let your self-worth be tied or limited by other people's perceptions of who they think you are no matter their level of seniority. Be your own judge of what you are worth.

- **Act from a place of truth even when you think no one is looking or you think the result is of no consequence.** Your environment is a reflection of your inner world. Acting from a place of untruth when you know in your heart that you are being dishonest or not speaking up when you should creates the energy for that untruth to reflect back into your life. You draw others to you who are in that same life state, and so the struggle to end suffering in the workplace becomes all the more challenging *for everyone*. Take bold action. As Gandhi said, *We need not wait to see what others would do.*[32]

"Tain't what you do; it's the way that you do it."

— ELLA FITZGERALD

#18

CREATE PSYCHOLOGICAL SAFETY

Psychological Safety :

the ability to express yourself without fear of adverse repercussions on image, social or professional standing, or career.

Can you recall a time when you kept quiet when you know you should have spoken up? When the benefit of zipping your lips outweighed the benefit of speaking up? Chances are, you remained silent because you feared the consequences.

The Volkswagen Story

In 2015, the US Environmental Protection Agency discovered that 482,000 Volkswagen diesel cars were emitting up to forty times more toxic fumes than allowed. They discovered that VW intentionally programmed their software so that engines activated emissions controls only during laboratory testing. VW later admitted this violation affected eleven million cars worldwide.

In order to meet their goal to bypass rivals General Motors and Toyota to become the world's largest automaker by the year 2018[33], VW leaders fostered a climate of fear and authoritarianism. Even executives feared interaction with the Volkswagen CEO. One admitted: "If he would come and visit or you had to go to him, your pulse would go up. If you presented bad news, those were the moments that it could become quite unpleasant and loud and quite demeaning.[34]"

A member of the supervisory board wrote to staff afterwards:

> "We need in future a climate in which problems aren't hidden but can be openly communicated to superiors. We need a culture in which it's possible and permissible to argue with your superior about the best way to go."

Volkswagen's stock price fell in value by a third in the days immediately after the news.

What can we learn from the Volkswagen scandal? Could this very expensive mistake have been averted had employees felt able to ask about or challenge a certain practice?

People need freedom to take risks, make mistakes, fail, and share opinions and ideas, without being criticized or reprimanded. They must feel that it's okay to address the elephant in the room. If they think a project is heading for disaster, or has some flaws in the process that could cause problems down the line, they should feel safe enough to share their perspective without things getting unpleasant. Yet, a recent Gallup poll highlights that just three in ten U.S. workers strongly agree that at work, their opinions seem to count.[35]

The best-performing teams, according to a Google study, are those in which members feel comfortable sharing ideas without fear of rebuke. These teams are better at implementing diverse ideas and driving high performance.[36] Google also found that sales teams with the highest levels of psychological safety outperformed their goal by an average of 17%, while those with the lowest levels of psychological safety missed their goals by an average of 19%.[37]

Sales teams with the HIGHEST levels of psychological safety OUTPERFORM their goals by an average of

17%

while those with the LOWEST levels of psychological safety MISS their goals by an average of

19%

The Bottom Line...

Facilitating environments that are safe spaces for people to speak, stick their necks out, and be heard, is critical to the open exploration of new thinking and innovations.

ACTION STEP

Creating psychological safety does not come down to doing one thing. It is a number of action steps that done in tandem will – over time – move the needle and allow you to generate deeper trust.

Keep the 3C's in mind:

Consistency

Creating psychological safety is not a one and done deal. 'Nuff said.

Communication

You have to have those courageous conversations and lay your feelings, needs and requests out on the table.

Care

You have to genuinely care. If you're checking a box with this one, you will go nowhere fast.

In addition, implement these three fundamentals:

1. Acknowledge Where Responsibility Lies

While leadership clearly has a role to play, their actions are not going to land with everyone all of the time. Individuals need to take responsibility for making sure their leaders understand what they need from them to feel psychologically safe – and to communicate when they don't. Have each person take responsibility for conducting a personal integrity check.

2. Provide And Seek Out Regular Feedback

In particular, listen when people talk. A lot of communication takes place non-verbally. Listen for the words (or lack of), listen for clues in tonality, and look out for body language that demonstrates someone is emotionally charged or has withdrawn.

3. Decentralize Power

Shift decision-making from leaders to teams. Some ideas will hit a home run, others will stink. Risk comes with the territory when you are breaking new ground. Learn how to evaluate and mitigate these risks rather than take away people's power and autonomy.

Remember: People support what they create.

"The test of our progress is not whether we add more to the abundance of those who have much; it is whether we provide enough for those who have too little."

— FRANKLIN D. ROOSEVELT

#19

CLOSE THE INEQUALITY GAP

Fact: Women Today Drive The World Economy.

Half of the world's population is female, yet women today are making, on average, eighty percent of the buying decisions. Women lead when it comes to deciding what homes and cars are bought, where the family vacations, what furnishings are bought, and what food is bought. Women control eighteen trillion dollars in annual consumer spending,[38] thirty-nine trillion dollars – or one third – of the world's wealth,[39] and we are still considered a largely untapped market.

Indeed, the growth market for women is more than 2X bigger than the growth markets of China and India combined.[40]

It stands to reason, then, that having more female CEOs, more women on boards, more women in C-suite, plus, harnessing the skills of female talent across all levels of the organization, would significantly enhance innovation and economic growth.

The Women In Leadership Challenge

In recent years, there has been a growing focus amongst big businesses to ensure there is diverse representation of women at both the board level and in the C-suite. Whether it is because legislation demands it, or because leaders believe this is morally the right thing to do, what does this actually mean for businesses that are looking to innovate and gain or maintain their competitive edge?

Companies in today's economy are competing ferociously for new ideas, and increasingly looking to sell into global markets and target new demographics as a strategy for increasing revenue. In order to develop innovative products that forge stronger connections with customers, they will need to engage and leverage their diverse talent and take steps to close the inequality gap. These should be front and center in any future-focused company's strategic planning going forward.

Diverse groups are better problem solvers

Researchers have found that diverse groups can solve problems better than more homogenous teams[41] and companies that are more ethnically and gender diverse performed significantly better than others.[42] When the backgrounds, experiences and perspectives of the people on your team are limited, so are the solutions that emerge. As a team, you will come up with fewer ideas and the ideas that are generated will sound the same. Having gender and cultural diversity improves team performance and can open up new markets, while making existing markets more profitable.

The IFC and BLC Bank of Lebanon Story

The International Finance Corporation (IFC) worked with the BLC Bank of Lebanon and engaged women in the product design process to more successfully target female consumers. By developing new products such as collateral-free loans, legal work-arounds that allowed women to open accounts for their children for the first time, and a suite of non-financial services for women entrepreneurs, BLC established itself as the bank of choice for women. As a result, **the initiative saw a healthy 33% internal rate of return**.[43]

Clearly, businesses are losing out on massive profit growth by not nurturing the talents of the women they employ.

This is what happens when women aren't given the same opportunities as men...

In the last few years, with all the drum-beating around gender equality in the workplace, one might wonder how leading companies with their big teams and even bigger budgets could make crazy blunders. However, when women aren't included in every step of the leadership, design, and delivery process, there have been a barrage of well-known brands that have missed the mark, and their attempts to speak to the female market have led to some epic fails...

The Bic Story

In 2015, Bic, the stationary company, was forced to remove their not-so-empowering Women's Day ad they ran on Facebook.

Look like a girl
Act like a lady
Think like a man
Work like a boss

The offensive undertones in the tagline outraged consumers and caused a social media outcry. Women fired back they were quite okay with looking like a woman, acting like a woman, thinking like a woman, and working like a woman.44

The Washington Post Express Story

In January 2017, the *Washington Post Express* illustrated its cover story on the Women's March in Washington using the Greek sign for Mars (to represent men) instead of the circle and cross to represent Venus (used to symbolize women).

Fast Company quickly branded this faux-pas **"the most epic design fail of the year"**45 and readers were quick to slam the *Washington Post Express* for their sexism and systemic bias as well as question if the *Express* had female editors on staff.

This is what happens when women aren't given adequate skills training when in leadership positions...

The Diageo Story

In 2018, when Diageo – the company that owns the Johnnie Walker brand – launched a limited-edition female version of its top-hat-wearing male icon, it **alienated at least 29% of its consumer audience.**[46] Even with female Vice President Stephanie Jacoby as its spokesperson in a media interview, the company managed to dig a bigger hole for itself. When Jacoby announced, "Scotch as a category is seen as particularly intimidating by women...It's a really exciting opportunity to invite women into the brand"[47] the public reacted harshly to her condescending words.

Diageo has since called upon advertising agencies to put forward at least one female director as part of any work pitch[48] but the kinds of mistakes that have taken place in the last few years tell us **it's not that easy to think differently, even when women are on the leadership team.** These failures suggest that having women represented at senior levels in an organization, and bringing more women into the pipeline through innovative recruiting strategies, while being a start, is not enough.

Closing The Inequality Gap

To help women be more successful at opening up new opportunities, lead into the next decade, and show their value in the workplace, companies need to **close the Inequality Gap**.

This involves addressing THREE key areas:

SKILLS PARITY
PAY PARITY
OPPORTUNITY PARITY

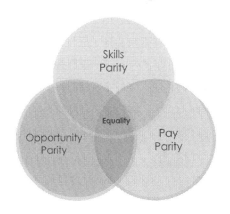

Parity:
the state of being equal.

Skills Parity:

A business' changing needs are matched by the skills possessed by the workforce.

With the workplace evolving and the push to place more women in C-suite or board-level positions, businesses have to look beyond hiring top female talent. They need to nurture their current pipeline and provide women with the skills and training to be able to win in their roles.

Here's an example of how addressing *Skills Parity* can lead to a win for women and a win for business:

Men are more likely to be *perceived* as risk-takers and women are *perceived* as more adaptive and risk-averse.[49] These perceptions create expectations which lead to a self-fulfilling prophecy: they perpetuate more innovative behavior in men and and more adaptive solutions from women. Indeed, research reveals that innovative solutions are more likely to be implemented if they are suggested by a male.[50]

These detrimental patterns can easily inhibit women from speaking up and sharing any blue sky ideas. In such a scenario, skills training would be invaluable in providing women with a systematic process for dreaming "bigger" and then sharing their bold ideas with others without fear of judgment.

Pay Parity:

Employees performing the same role in the same location are paid fairly to one another.

Women are currently paid eighty cents to the dollar for performing the same role as a man, and at the current rate of progress, the gender pay gap won't close until 2119 – exactly one hundred years from now.[51]

Families today are increasingly relying on women's wages to meet basic expenses and 42% of women in the workforce have sole responsibility for supporting their families. Many working women are mothers which means they are typically juggling career with childcare commitments. And with their lesser salaries, they carry student debt for longer than men also.[52]

All of this adds to financial instability, and the pressure this puts on women to wear multiple hats without rocking the boat is great. This cannot be good for the growth of any business, and it smacks innovative behavior in the face.

In *Un-habit Yourself*, we talked about how when the body is under stress, our ability to form new connections and apply new knowledge is reduced. How many women will dare to break the rules when faced with this kind of pressure? Indeed, maintaining the status quo and not taking action on addressing gender pay parity in your company prevents women from speaking up, discussing the unmentionable, and using their talents to show up as strong, courageous leaders – the antithesis of what this book is about.

Opportunity Parity:

Fair and equal opportunities for all demographic groups to grow, develop, move, and advance within an organization.

There are two plays that will open up opportunities for employees within your company. They are:

- a **lateral move** into a different role in the organization – perhaps one that is better suited to an individual's strengths, interests, or longer-term career goals.

- an **internal promotion** whereby an individual moves into a role with more scope, challenge, responsibility, and impact.

Creating *Opportunity Parity* includes giving people an avenue –

- to be mentored by someone – formally or informally – who they can learn from.
- to step into a role that better aligns employer-employee needs.
- to step into a role that challenges them in a different way.

When we are performing a role that we are not happy in, our mind and body pay the price. Our brain shuts down responsiveness to information – which in turns renders us less effective and productive.

Leaders: this workplace innovation is good for the company *and* the individual – it prevents you from losing good employees and keeps everyone engaged and giving their best.

ACTION STEP

To Address Skills Parity:

- Address any mismatch between your business' changing needs and the skills possessed by the women in your team or workforce.
- Ensure women (and other under represented groups) have access to skills training specific to their needs and unique challenges.
- Be proactive in up-skilling women for current roles.
- Get women "next level leadership-ready" by providing training opportunities and exposure to environments and skills outside their role, responsibilities, and expertise.

To Address Pay Parity:

- Implement – and adhere to – clear policies and guidelines against gender pay gaps.
- Conduct – or request – that a company-wide pay gap audit be conducted.
- Ensure salaries are reviewed on an annual basis for consistency and fairness.
- Correct any discrepancies immediately.

To Address Opportunity Parity:

- Give employees, without bias or discrimination, equal access to learning and development opportunities.
- Incorporate coaching and feedback mechanisms into team conversations to understand the unique struggles women are experiencing.
- Learn about team members short-term and long-term aspirations with regards to career advancement and lateral moves within the organization.
- Be plugged into the company's evolving needs and availability of roles so that you can open doors and make recommendations where appropriate.

Your business' growth will be stunted or boosted by your level of commitment to closing the inequality gap. Supporting women in developing skills to prepare for the seismic shift that is taking place, addressing pay differences, running an audit *even if you don't think inequality exists in your firm*, and giving them access to opportunities where they are thriving and the company is benefiting...all of this is a triple win; a win for the individuals, a win for your company, and a win for the cause.

Be rigorous in ensuring a level playing field and be transparent in your findings and the changes you are making. While change doesn't happen overnight, when your employees know you are committed to making fairness a top priority, it generates enormous goodwill. And when you generate employee goodwill, you also garner loyalty, respect, hustle, and creativity. **Closing the inequality gap is a force multiplier.**

"If I were again beginning my studies, I would follow the advice of Plato and start with mathematics."

— GALILEO GALILEI

#20

LEVERAGE THE X-CATCHER

When I was a kid, math was like zen. It was enchanting and fun and relaxing, and I relished the challenge. Over time, I'd push myself to do complex math homework in pen...that was me living dangerously!

I would pride myself on figuring out long and complicated algebra calculations on the back of a napkin – i.e. sans calculator – thinking that solving x was a profound universal problem and the key to creating order out of chaos. It turns out I wasn't far from the truth.

In old naval slang, an X-catcher or X-chaser was someone who was good at math[53] – literally, someone good at working out the value of x. ('X' being the unknown in algebraic equations).

In today's age, this represents someone who can take complex data and work out how it translates into a measurable ROI – **i.e. someone who catches the *x* and turns it into dollars that will make your CFO sing.**

"Our company just went through a round of layoffs and I was one of the people they let go. I never set up the ROI with the projects I had spearheaded and so, given the financial challenges they are facing, it was a relatively easy decision for them to make the cut in my department. In hindsight, I realize how vital it was to demonstrate that our initiatives made good business sense.

– Jessica, Head of Product Development

Imagine you have a new idea for a product. Or, you are asked to submit a proposal with your ideas on how to expand an initiative you currently oversee. Or, perhaps you are in charge of designing a training day in which you are bringing your global leaders from four continents together to brainstorm and come up with a unified Diversity, Equity, and Inclusion strategy.

For any of these scenarios, your leadership team will be looking for breakthrough ideas, strategies, and approaches that generate a return on the investment made – whether that investment was time, money, or something else.

X-catchers thrive in this space.

They don't toss around goals that sound soft, abstract, or nebulous.

They integrate a process for articulating and measuring the impact with detailed quantifiable financial results that command stakeholder attention.

One of the ways we leverage the *X*-catchers in our firm is helping clients turn abstract goals into concrete ones. We dig deep by asking clients a lot of questions before defining goals, objectives, and outcomes. We then measure their progress at strategic points along the way so they know if they are on course or if adjustments need to be made. This prevents new initiatives going off the rails.

After a project is complete, we are able to clearly articulate – with the numbers to back them up – how it has affected the bottom line. C-suite executives, in particular, really appreciate this because they can see the impact on their investment every step of the way. Our in-house *X*-catchers will incorporate this into any large scale projects we implement as part of the service that we offer to our clients. It gives executives confidence that they made the right choice in partnering with us.

10 WAYS TO LEVERAGE AN X-CATCHER

1. Win more business from your partners and customers
2. Gain budget approvals / increases
3. Be better positioned to keep the business and client loyalty you've generated
4. Be better positioned to keep the budget you have been allocated
5. Generate marketing / PR buzz
6. Negotiate salary increases

7. Gain deeper insights and support strategic planning process

8. Hedge against volatility and respond faster to leading change

9. Prevent profit from falling between the operational cracks

10. Demonstrate value to your peers and leadership team (which increases their perception of the value *you* deliver)

Remember: You need to know the value of X

- **Before you make an investment**...to ensure it is worth your while).

- **At strategic mid-way points**...to ensure you are on track.

- **Afterwards**...so that you can capitalize on your initiatives and achievements.

Ideas are great. Execution rocks. Knowing the ROI amplifies the contributions of everyone involved and keeps stakeholders happy.

ACTION STEP

To turn your data into dollars, **identify the X-catchers** in your team and within firms that you partner with on any large project. The *X*-catcher's zone of genius is to help you gather and make sense of the data, translate it into a ROI, and highlight or 'catch' what you may have missed.

"What if I don't have an X-catcher on my team?"

It could be that you don't have an *X*-catcher in your team or division. In this case, you have two options:

- **Learn** how to run calculations on the monetary value of a new project or initiative.
- **Partner** with a firm that can take ownership of this essential piece of the innovation puzzle.

Larger companies that mine data to make strategic operational decisions typically have skilled data analysts on board – but oftentimes, the job of translating value in monetary terms is left to a division head or project lead.

If this is you, here are 10 things to think about to get you started:

1. *What impact will **X** have on you?*
2. *What impact will **X** have on your division? Your organization? Your industry?*
3. *Will **X** create a domino effect? If so, how?*
4. *What are the advantages of putting **X** into place?*
5. *What is the cost if you don't put **X** into place?*
6. *What have others done?*
7. *What is the industry standard?*
8. *What are you saving, growing, increasing, reducing, improving, speeding up, simplifying?*
9. *What will be different as a result?*
10. *How are you going to measure the value of **X**?*

If you'd like our help with turning your data into dollars and effectively incorporating this information into a growth strategy, reach out. We walk our clients through our proprietary ROI process step-by-step *so that you can see it in action.* **X**-cellente!

"Before you can think out of the box, you have to start with a box."

— TWLYA THARP

#21

THINK INSIDE THE BOX

When people talk about thinking differently or unconventionally, the expression *think outside the box* often springs to mind. It's become almost cliché – a kind of bumper sticker slogan that is well-worn in business circles. For every three companies my firm works with, at least one person internally will, at some point, say to me: *You're really helping us think outside the box.* Yet few understand that the reason they are succeeding during our sessions is because I am actually teaching them to think *inside* the box.

To think outside the box is a lofty goal and a hard one. Let's look at the concept more closely to understand why.

Thinking outside the box is about confronting challenges in atypical ways. The phrase became popular after management consultants in the 1970s and 1980s challenged their clients to solve the *Nine Dots* puzzle in order to develop lateral thinking.

The Nine ~~Dots~~ Squares Puzzle

Below are nine squares arranged in a set of three rows.

(Sidenote: The original puzzle was in the form of dots. I am innovating on this as I write. Did you know that the period in certain fonts is actually a square? I didn't – until I blew this one up to size 144! Yah Yah. So, technically, typeface designer Max Miedinger innovated this period. I am innovating on the puzzle. Demonstrates my point: all ideas come from within a box. Even if it's someone else's box.)

Okay, back to the puzzle. I'll call mine the *Nine Squares Puzzle*.

The challenge is to draw four straight lines which go through the middle of each of the squares without taking the pen off the paper.

Go ahead. See if you can solve it.

Did you do it?

To accomplish it, you'd have to cross boundaries, or draw outside the dots (or squares). Here's one possible solution:

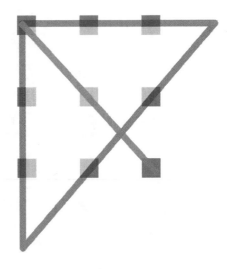

Not obvious, right? Harvard Business School professor, Francesca Gino, ran a study of more than two thousand employees in a variety of industries and found that fewer than 10% said that they worked in firms that encouraged nonconformity or thinking outside the box.[54]

It's no wonder. **Asking people to think outside the box i.e. without any limitations, flings open the door to an infinite number of options. It feels daunting. For some, it can even be paralyzing.**

So what does it mean to...

*Think **INSIDE** The Box?*

Dig Deep: Overcoming the Chicken and the Egg in Sales

A client approached me to design a gamulation around networking and relationship building for a sales conference breakout session. To accomplish this, I talked to a senior leader about the challenges his business unit were experiencing while building relationships.

"In the short term, we want to make the sale," he told me. "However, we may not close the deal or win any future business if we don't spend enough time building long-term relationships. Can you design something to help the team with this?"

This leader was right on the money. We can spend hours and hours of time with prospects taking them out to lunches and dinners and ball games, but if we haven't taken the time to learn about their likes, dislikes, spouses and pets, then there won't be much depth to the relationship, and therefore little trust built.

But in a professional setting, what's appropriate and what's not? What kind of questions can you ask that will really help you dig deep and learn about a person in a short period of time without sounding generic, or worse, crossing inappropriate boundaries??

I've found that many people struggle with this – even salespeople who love to talk!

Salespeople have been conditioned over the years to be hunters and many have forgotten the art of real relationship building. So I created a training to help attendees overcome this roadblock.

To set them up for success, I created parameters. No pie-in-the-sky, open-ended instructions like: *Mingle with folks around the room and ask questions so that you can really get to know them. Think outside the box!* I've been to networking events where I've been told this. I often wished the floor would open up and swallow me whole.

Instead, I created a "box" for them to step into – or what I call the **Rules Of Play**. The rules when you are inside the box are simple: (1) Participants can only pick questions to ask people out of the twenty-five I had given them, and (2) They had to listen to the response given without interruption.

I then gave them the questions and **invited them all to think (play) inside the box.**

How do you fill your space?	How do you spend your time?	How do you spend your energy?	How do you spend your money?	Where are you most energized?
Where are you most reliable?	What do you most often talk to others about?	What dominates your thoughts?	What do you visualize most?	What do you most often talk to yourself about?
What inspires you?	What goals stand out in your life and have stood the test of time?	What do you love to learn or read about most?	Why did you choose to come and live in this city?	Share a favorite quote and why it is meaningful to you.
Describe something that gives you joy?	Share one quality about yourself that you love.	Share something unique about yourself, your family, or your heritage?	What do you like to do in your downtime?	Describe something difficult you have overcome in your life.
Name a person that has impacted your life and explain how.	Find one thing you have in common with each other.	Describe the first time that you fell in love.	What one thought keeps you up at night?	What do you want your legacy to be?

The Result

The feedback was overwhelmingly positive. People reported back that they learned things about their colleagues they hadn't discovered over the many years of working with them. They reported that at first they were hesitant to ask what seemed like very personal questions because it was a professional setting and these were professional relationships.

Yet, they played by the rules and discovered during the process that it is okay to get personal and real, and to share with colleagues that other side to us that we typically keep hidden from most of the world.

The *Rules Of Play* – or box – that I had set up kept everyone engaged while keeping the atmosphere lighthearted and playful. Once everyone knew what was in the box, the fear went away and they had a lot of fun getting to know each other in a more personal way. **This led to them being able to think outside the box** with how they would approach client relationship building in the future.

The takeaway? These groups simply needed constraints to be able to set them free. Without the pressure of having to come up with what to ask, or asking something stupid and risk looking foolish, they had the freedom to take a chance with a new approach, have fun with the challenge, and learn something.

ACTION STEP

Create A Box.

In order to expand your creative potential as a leader and innovator, you need to start with a box. Think of a box as a tool that gives your ideas structure and enables you to get to where you want to get to faster – much like scaffolding does for a building. The box can be a Word document on your computer, a mind-map, an actual physical box, or it can be a concept that you apply to the creative process.

To decide what *your* box looks like, think about your objective.

Here are some ideas of how leaders of our time have used thinking *inside* the box to drive innovation:

I want to write a new song on a new topic.

George Harrison, lead guitarist of the Beatles, created a constraint: he would pick up a book, open it, then write a song about whatever words he read first. He read the words "gently weeps" and wrote the song "While My

Guitar Gently Weeps" – long considered one of his best songs.

We want to create a new, user-friendly product.

The iPhone was developed with one constraint: One Button.

We want to build a community where people can share opinions.

Quora built a platform with one constraint: Start with a Question.

I want people to order our product the moment they realize they need it.

The constraint Amazon placed on themselves? The ability to place orders without access to a phone or computer. Their *inside-the-box* solution? The Dash Button. Customers can place the button anywhere where they use a particular product. When they run out of a product, they press the Dash Button and two days later it arrives on their doorstep. No need to wait to open the app. No need to add to the cart. No need to go through the checkout process.

I want readers to find my ideas easy to implement.

When I started the process of writing this book, I started with one constraint: the ideas must inspire action.
My solution: End every chapter with an action step.

Remember: Conventional thinking teaches us that constraints fetter the creative mind. The big advantage of working within strict constraints is that it will FOCUS your thinking. Thinking *inside* the box is about creating parameters that limit the scope. It will fire up the problem-solving part of the brain to fill your empty box with new ideas, and work to find a solution.

Thinking *inside* the box will unleash a creativity within you, you never knew you had.

Now get ready. Because the ideas, visions, thoughts, plans, and more, will come pouring like an avalanche.

SECTION II:

TAKING ACTION

WHAT TO DO NEXT

Have you ever experienced excitement for something and then have it quickly turn into overwhelm? For me, and many others I talk to, when we experience overwhelm, something in our calendar – or in our life – has to get parked.

Sadly, what this frequently means, is that when we look back at things in three months, six months, one year from today...we observe that little has changed...

How often have you seen senior leaders challenge the status quo or ask employees to think outside the box? [54]

This is the question Francesca Gino put to the over two thousand employees in her study.

The responses were as follows:

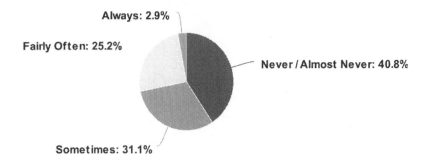

What she discovered is that while many leaders in search of the next big thing often get excited about the idea of leading change, spearheading growth, and challenging the status quo, they end up *not taking action*.

To prevent this,

Take This ONE Step Next

TURN THE SPOTLIGHT OF ACCOUNTABILITY ON YOURSELF

Taking responsibility and holding yourself (and others) accountable requires work – especially when it comes to dipping your toes in new territory.

How to do this?

It's as easy as 1-2-3...

1. ACKNOWLEDGE what you don't know.

Not everyone is going to be an expert at everything. Have a beginner's mind. Be humble and open.

2. Take just ONE idea in this book and IMPLEMENT it.

Track your progress, and measure your results. Then test out another idea. While you won't strike gold with every strategy, think of yourself as a business athlete getting ready for a mini-marathon rather than a sprint. You are training your mind to think differently. This is a skill in and of itself. Once you master this, you will be able to apply it to most any situation and be more adept at solving bigger problems faster than others.

3. *ASK for help.*

Look again at the pie chart on a previous page demonstrating the results of Gino's study.

You are not alone. Work in teams to give and receive feedback on the ideas that resonate the most with you. When you get stuck or when you want to fast-track your journey, seek the advice of an outside expert or reach out to someone who is two steps ahead of you. Everyone needs a mentor, a coach, and a cheerleader on their team.

ARE YOU A LION OR A SHEEP?

"I am not afraid of an army of lions led by a sheep; I am afraid of an army of sheep led by a lion."

– *Alexander The Great*

This book is designed to be your guide and innovation companion; twenty-one diverse ideas, loaded with stories of diverse leaders from diverse industries, with the goal of opening up your mind to think differently. You will raise your innovation IQ by seeing your business challenges through a fresh lens, applying new strategies, broadening your horizons, and looking beyond your own company and your current role for the answers. With diligent application, the *21 ways to think differently during times of change* we have covered here will help you bust through your roadblocks and breakthrough into new territory.

I hope that as you were reading, you were connecting the dots across the chapters. In today's economy, raising your innovation IQ is not just about product and process innovation. Businesses everywhere are prioritizing innovating corporate culture, employees' career paths, indeed, their entire business strategy. In today's economy, raising your innovation IQ is not just about generating leading-edge ideas; it is equally as important to be able to execute on these ideas so they deliver a solid return on investment. And in today's economy, raising your innovation IQ is not just about making a profit, it is about putting people at the forefront and running your business in a conscious way – with regard for the ripple effect you are creating in the community and in the world. To lead yourself and others in this, you have to bring your A-game; your whole self to the table – mentally, physically, emotionally, and spiritually. The word *gestalt* comes to mind once again.

This book is about expanding the concept of innovation so that it applies to every nook and cranny of your business /career / life /world. I want you to succeed not just in thinking differently so that you can raise your innovation IQ, be a better leader, and skillfully navigate the future. I want you to succeed at this because it is *who you are meant to be.*

You, too, were once a six-year-old kid who made crazy connections between chocolate ice cream and who knows what! Stop checking a big chunk of yourself, your experiences, and your life story at the door when you start the work day. Be wary of the perils of not questioning the status quo, following others blindly like sheep, and not saying what's on your mind when necessary.

Bring the big kid in you out to play more often. Take the sandbox into the boardroom and invite others in your team to think inside the box. Stay curious, imaginative, weird, daring, playful, and open because it's these very qualities that have spurred every innovation that we consider standard today.

When we take responsibility for how we move through life, no matter our circumstances, we become like lions; with one roar we allow our personal power to be fully expressed. If we are able to live in this way – like lions instead of sheep – we become magnets who inspire and give permission to others to become leaders in *their* lives.

Our impact is not defined by the people who we know, but by the people who know about us and are moved by our presence in their world.

Go forth. Live boldly. Express yourself fully. Create new boxes, new hypotheses, new approaches, new solutions.

Train yourself so that you are not just raising your innovation IQ for today and tomorrow, but for the next decade.

THE ~~END~~ BEGINNING...

LAUNCHING A NEW INITIATIVE?

If you are launching (or exploring launching) a new initiative in the next 30-45 days and would like a few additional insights that would be particularly helpful to you in this phase, reach out.

WANT TO SHARE A STORY FOR THE NEXT EDITION?
MAKE A COMMENT?

Meet Leena at:
www.Sandbox2Boardroom.com

ENDNOTES

[1] EY, Top Priorities For Boards In 2019 Report,4

[2] https://www.fastcompany.com/most-innovative-companies/2019

[3] https://www.fastcompany.com/most-innovative-companies/2018

[4] https://medium.com/accelerated-intelligence/modern-polymath-81f882ce52db

[5] https://www.newspapers.com/clip/13442917/halitosis_makes_you_unpopular_use/

[6] https://www.kelloggs.com/en_US/who-we-are/our-history.html

[7] https://www.3m.com/3M/en_US/sustainability-report/all-stories/full-story/~15-percent-time-innovation/?storyid=c871812b-1aec-45c3-9b1f-79104cf82f78

[8] https://news.3m.com/press-release/company/3m-celebrates-innovation-milestone-receives-100000th-patent

[9] https://neurosciencenews.com/learning-memory-emotion-limbic-system-2393/

[10] https://www.adweek.com/digital/you-cant-be-creative-without-data/

[11] https://disney.fandom.com/wiki/Three_Men_and_a_Baby

[12] https://gointothestory.blcklst.com/would-studios-return-to-the-singles-and-doubles-approach-to-making-movies-aa3b76f15148

[13] https://www.washingtonpost.com/world/obama-lays-out-his-foreign-policy-doctrine-singles-doubles-and-the-occasional-home-run/2014/04/28/e34ec058-ceb5-11e3-937f-d3026234b51c_story.html

[14] https://fameable.com/diamond-shreddies-rebranding-case-study/144/

[15] https://www.adweek.com/creativity/these-bite-size-horror-films-from-mars-candy-brands-are-the-best-halloween-ads-in-years/

[16] https://www.adweek.com/creativity/these-bite-size-horror-films-from-mars-candy-brands-are-the-best-halloween-ads-in-years/

[17] https://www.thoughtco.com/history-of-post-it-note-1992326

[18] Oppezzo, M., & Schwartz, D. L. (2014). Give your ideas some legs: The positive effect of walking on creative thinking. Journal of Experimental Psychology: Learning, Memory, and Cognition, 40(4), 1142-1152.

19 https://www.forbes.com/sites/karagoldin/2018/04/20/why-meetings-on-the-move-should-be-the-new-normal-and-how-to-ensure-theyre-productive/#30a7131b5668

20 https://www.ncbi.nlm.nih.gov/pmc/articles/PMC3845014/

21 http://fortune.com/2011/11/15/silicon-valleys-different-kind-of-power-walk/

22 "What May Happen in the Next Hundred Years" by John Elfreth Watkins. Ladies' Home Journal" magazine, December 1900, page 8

23 https://www.nytimes.com/2008/10/23/business/worldbusiness/23iht-gspan.4.17206624.html

24 http://thescienceexplorer.com/technology/9-most-mind-blowing-things-elon-musk-believes

25 https://www.corning.com/media/worldwide/global/documents/Creating-an-innovation-culture.pdf

26 http://yalecollege.yale.edu/sites/default/files/files/woodward_report.pdf

27 https://www.raconteur.net/business-innovation/collaboration-is-good-for-business

28 https://hbr.org/2016/01/collaborative-overload

29 http://smallbizlink.monster.com/news/articles/897-apple-we-say-no-to-good-ideas-every-day

30 https://www.youtube.com/watch?v=ItimoPxkxZI

31 https://www.toledoblade.com/business/development/2019/03/14/ups-workers-recall-nooses-other-racist-acts-at-maumee-facility/stories/20190314100

32 Morton, B. (2014). Opinion | Falser Words Were Never Spoken. nytimes.com

33 https://www.thetruthaboutcars.com/2010/02/volkswagen's-strategy-2018-with generous-support-from-gm-and-toyota

34 https://www.reuters.com/article/uk-volkswagen-emissions-culture/fear-and-respect-vws-culture-under-winterkorn-idUKKCN0S40MN20151010

35 https://www.gallup.com/workplace/236198/create-culture-psychological-safety.aspx

36 https://www.inc.com/leigh-buchanan/most-productive-teams-at-google.html

37 https://www.nytimes.com/2016/02/28/magazine/what-google-learned-from-its-quest-to-build-the-perfect-team.html?_r=1

[38] https://www.forbes.com/sites/bridgetbrennan/2015/01/21/top-10-things-everyone-should-know-about-women-consumers/#3482afe96a8b

[39] https://www.bcg.com/publications/2016/financial-institutions-consumer-insight-global-wealth-2016.aspx

[40] https://www.forbes.com/sites/bridgetbrennan/2015/01/21/top-10-things-everyone-should-know-about-women-consumers/#3482afe96a8b

[41] https://sites.lsa.umich.edu/scottepage/wp-content/uploads/sites/344/2015/11/pnas.pdf

[42] McKinsey&Company, Why Diversity Matters, 2015 report,1

[43] https://www.ifc.org/wps/wcm/connect/f24d9b5f-855e-4502-a771-8f2f1c95c21b/Case+Study+BLC+Bank+Lebanon_31082016.pdf?MOD=AJPERES

[44] https://www.independent.co.uk/news/world/bic-apologises-for-sexist-think-like-a-man-advert-designed-to-celebrate-south-africa-womens-day-10449842.html

[45] https://www.fastcompany.com/3066980/ladies-and-gentlemen-the-biggest-design-fail-of-2017

[46] https://www.entrepreneur.com/article/309990

[47] https://www.forbes.com/sites/brianfreedman/2018/02/27/diageos-new-jane-walker-scotch-bottles-are-a-risky-attempt-to-appeal-to-women/#21553fc3ef1a

[48] https://sites.lsa.umich.edu/scottepage/wp-content/uploads/sites/344/2015/11/pnas.pdf

[49] Gender Differences in Risk Assessment: Why do Women Take Fewer Risks than Men? Judgment and Decision Making, Vol. 1, No. 1, July 2006, pp. 48–63

[50] https://www.tandfonline.com/doi/abs/10.1207/S15326934CRJ1401_8#.Uac-z-vyo7o

[51] https://www.aauw.org/research/the-simple-truth-about-the-gender-pay-gap/

[52] https://www.debt.com/news/women-have-more-student-loan-debt-than-men/

[53] http://mentalfloss.com/article/70959/words-that-start-with-x

[54] Francesco Gino, Let Your Workers Rebel https://hbr.org/cover-story/2016/10/let-your-workers-rebel

Leena Patel is the founder of Sandbox2Boardroom.com and a leading expert on helping executive teams worldwide lead change, drive innovation, and develop a winning culture of creativity, collaboration, and inclusion. She partners with big businesses and fast-growing companies to design and execute on innovation initiatives that capitalize on new business opportunities and secure a strategic market position.

Recognized with a Smart Woman Innovator Award and Woman of Distinction Award for pioneering *Gamulation* as a revolutionary leadership training methodology, Leena and her team have worked with leading corporations in 16+ industries, advised CEOs and Senior Executives worldwide, delivered over 1000 seminars, and have been featured by leading media like NBC, Bloomberg, Fox News, ESPN, and many more.